Praise for *Which Way Is North*

"In a world of intersectionality, Cady masterfully explores the relationship between all the many pieces that make up who we are and helps us reassemble them to become who we are meant to be."

—Dr. Marcus Collins, Head of Strategy,
Wieden+Kennedy New York; Professor, Ross School of Business,
University of Michigan; and Author of *For the Culture*

"*Which Way Is North* is a deeply fascinating read. It draws from the author's own struggle to combine creativity, marketing, and spirituality—including the times in his life and career where those three fields seemed like embarrassments to each other. Cady invites the reader on a journey across media plans and meditations to show how creativity, marketing, and spirituality can inform and nourish each other, rather than conflict.

The narrative structure beautifully reflects the story as it's based on the meditation framework Cady uses as a blueprint for creative strategy. That brings the message off the page and into life—I found myself inspired to approach marketing and branding in new, more generous ways.

This is a brave and important book, exploring where creativity comes from and how to generate it, and inviting marketeers to use more of ourselves across all areas of life."

—Lea Sandell, Global Social Media Strategy, The LEGO Group

"Will Cady has a beautiful, unique, and inspiring way of seeing the world. With an exceptional ability to harmonize intellect and instinct, he offers us a transformative exploration of the human condition. Navigating some of the most profound questions of existence, Will's compelling insights will undoubtedly empower readers to discover their hidden potential and elevate their creative process."

—Nicholai Baxter, five-time Grammy Winner and Music
Producer for *CODA*, *La La Land*, *A Star Is Born*, *Maestro*,
The Color Purple, and *A Complete Unknown*

"For years, Will has been bringing his heart and soul to Reddit and helping businesses do the same. He's the perfect person to write a book like this. Every page offers a unique idea, valuable framing of a familiar feeling, or new view of the world."

—Steve Huffman, Cofounder and CEO, Reddit

"Will, affectionately known as the Shaman of Reddit, has beautifully translated the work he does every day into a must-read book for anyone seeking to tap into their creative potential. *Which Way Is North* serves as a valuable navigation tool, helping us to understand the complex yet cleverly simple world in which we live. Through a combination of personal stories, insightful essays, and practical meditations, Cady guides readers on a journey of self-discovery to find their True North. By bridging two seemingly disparate cultures—marketing and magic—Will's teachings allow each of us to navigate the challenges of art, business, and life with clarity, authenticity, and purpose. We all need a voice to guide our visions through the chaos. Will Cady is that voice."

—Katelin Holloway, Founding Partner, 776

"I'm grateful to have met Will early in our time together during the Reddit turnaround, and he's someone I always enjoy being around because I'm always learning something new about myself, the industry, or even the universe. I wish I'd had *Which Way Is North* as a companion when I was first creating Reddit, because I believe it would've helped me not only build a better product but also be a better leader. I've always fancied myself as a creator, but never had the words to properly articulate it, nor had I found the business tools that I felt spoke to me and my own process. Now I do. And I hope you indulge in this book not just the first time you read it, but revisit it for many years to come as you go on your own creative and spiritual journey."

—Alexis Ohanian, Founder, 776

"Will is one of those rare people who leads with his heart, mind, and spirituality front and center. With that framing, *Which Way Is North* is a must-read for anyone trying to help restore the soul of business today and look deeper at the buzzwords marketers hide behind, like 'authenticity' and 'empathy,' so you can connect on a deeper level and supercharge your human creativity."

—Denise Roberson, Chief Purpose Officer, TBWA\Chiat\Day

"At the intersection point of Adam Grant and Don Miguel Ruiz sits Will Cady and his mind/heart-opening book, *Which Way is North*. Cady's inaugural work is a mystical road map aimed at guiding fellow travelers and newbies alike toward creative enlightenment and actualizing their truest selves. In these noisy and volatile times, voices like Cady's serve as a bright, shining lighthouse amid a cyclone. Stay calm, my friends, and follow the light."

—Farhoud Meybodi, Founder, Ritual Arts

"A soulful exploration of the human experience, *Which Way Is North* takes on one of the defining cultural hallmarks of our time—our anxiety—and lights a pathway forward for all of us. In an era of unrelenting change and disruption, Will Cady—who will soon become your favorite maker, marketer, and mystic—teaches us how to find peace in the tumult and unlock our potential. A world-class musician from Berklee, a meditation guru, and a creative brand strategist all in one, Will Cady's *Which Way Is North* is an extension of his unique interdisciplinary life experiences. In this era of unease and disquiet, Cady's *Which Way Is North* can help us transform our anxiety into our creative superpower."

—Phillip Schermer, Founder and CEO, Project Healthy Minds

"Will has a truly unique ability to draw pathways between worlds and ideas that haven't traditionally been connected. As someone who is so deeply in tune with spirituality and cutting-edge culture and technology, he brings a modern approach and a thoughtful sensibility to everything he touches—a true modern-day spiritual guide. Will's ideas, techniques, and teachings are rooted in ancient wisdom, but reimagined to relate to the quickly changing world around us, making this book an indispensable guide for creatives, both new and seasoned, and one that you'll want to revisit time and time again."

—Leslie Kirchhoff, author, DJ, photographer, and Founder, Disco Cubes

"I recently had the pleasure of reading my friend Will Cady's book, *Which Way Is North*, and it's a game-changer for anyone looking to unlock their creativity. As someone who has had the opportunity to collaborate with Will over many years, and witnessed his boundless creativity firsthand, I can attest to the fact that he truly knows what he's talking about. In the book, Will shares a personal memoir, essays, and meditations that offer a unique perspective on creativity that will help you explore your inner experience and become conscious participants in the creation process. I especially appreciate the way he shares his modern meditation system to unlock intuition and ingenuity, something that has helped me personally in both my professional and personal life. With *Which Way Is North* as your guide, you'll gain practical tools to transform anxiety into creativity and find your inner authentic truths. I highly recommend this book to anyone looking to tap into their creative potential and embrace a more fulfilling life."

—Toby Daniels, Founder, ON_Discourse

"An engaging, easy to read, easy to understand, easy to follow road map that helps the reader uncover their true creative potential, and then guides them through a system that facilitates the reader's discovery of what they truly want their next 'life creation' to be."

—Jeff Segal, Owner and Founder, Mystic Journey Bookstore

"*Which Way Is North* is a must-read for conscious creatives seeking a holistic way to transform culture and change the world. Will Cady offers a visionary road map of the creative process, complete with the mystic, magical, and mindful technologies needed to traverse it. His vision of how to harmoniously shape culture is refreshing, inspiring, and empowering to makers of all kinds."

—Shaman Nabeel Redwood, Founder, Shamanic Healing LA, and author of *Inner Peace: A Shamanic Guide to Living Your Purpose*

"Will Cady's book, *Which Way is North*, is a perfect blend of the poetic and the practical. It's filled with dreamy stories and mindful meditations but still grounded in a day-to-day wisdom that makes the content feel both inspiring and eminently useful. We're all doing our best these days to find our purpose in a structured world—to find a balance in these complex times. Will's insights and offerings have allowed me to see a way to integrate all my creative facets—maker, mystic and marketer—into my everyday life with aplomb and grace."

—Dave Zaboski, Cofounder and Chief Creative Officer, Laetro, and former Senior Animator, Walt Disney Feature Animation

"He had me at 'being a spiritual guide' for the executives at Reddit. First of all, who knew Reddit had executives? If ever there was an asylum seemingly run by the lunatics it is, gloriously, Reddit. Furthermore, this book is genuinely about the creative process, which Cady understands so well, and the good news that creativity really does lurk, in some way, in everyone."

—Bob Guccione Jr., Founder/EIC of WONDERLUST and Founder of *SPIN*

WHICH WAY IS NORTH

A Creative Compass for Makers, Marketers, and Mystics

WILL CADY

Matt Holt Books
An Imprint of BenBella Books, Inc.
Dallas, TX

Matt Holt is an imprint of BenBella Books, Inc.
10440 N. Central Expressway
Suite 800
Dallas, TX 75231
benbellabooks.com
Send feedback to feedback@benbellabooks.com

BenBella and *Matt Holt* are federally registered trademarks.

Printed in the United States of America
10 9 8 7 6 5 4 3 2 1

Library of Congress Control Number: 2023007807
ISBN 9781637744062 (hardcover)
ISBN 9781637744079 (electronic)

Editing by Gregory Newton Brown
Copyediting by Michael Fedison
Proofreading by Denise Pangia and Cape Cod Compositors, Inc.
Text design and composition by PerfecType, Nashville, TN
Cover design by Brigid Pearson
Cover and interior compass illustrations by Dante Orpilla
Printed by Lake Book Manufacturing

Special discounts for bulk sales are available. Please contact bulkorders@benbellabooks.com.

To Rachelle Cady:

All the wonders
I seek to describe,
you already are.

A MAP

THE HEAD

DIRECTION I
GROWING | What Is in Front of You

DIRECTION VII
THE HEART | The Creative Journey

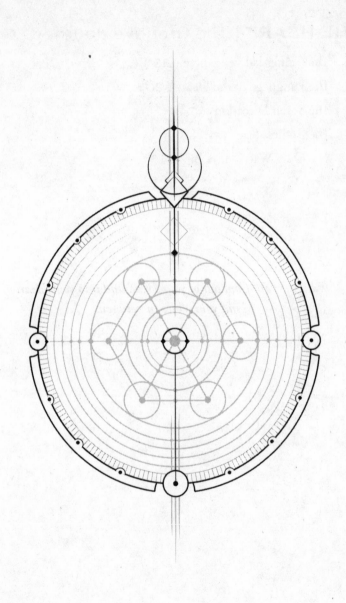

Walk the path from out of your Head and into your Heart.
Find your Voice in between.

Where Does Creativity Come From?

A POINT

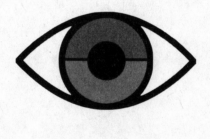

A VISION

A COMPASS

A STAR

A JOURNEY

A LESSON

THE HEAD

A Point

Anxiety Is Creativity Ready to Be Transmuted

A point starts somewhere.

We all struggle with creation, because creation *is* struggle. That is life's magic. The kind that sings beyond paint on canvas or words on a page. The big bang, magnificent and explosive, began everything with a defiant thrust of fire and formed into an empty expanse. A tiny sprout, with soft and steadfast resolution, pushes aside grains of soil to proudly share its first green leaves with the light. A mother pushes, sharing cries with her child, who will carry their story onward for the rest of their days. These are all accomplishments of creation.

It's been said that necessity is the mother of invention. If that is so, then perhaps anxiety is the father of creation. Experiencing struggle means you have its spark within you. Follow the light of that spark inward, and you may find that whatever seems to take your power, gives it. The weaknesses you carry might become your strength. The obstacles blocking you might become your guides through hidden pathways. That is transmutation in action.

I have met many people, myself included, who have been paralyzed by not knowing what to do with the discomfort of anxiety. Anxiety is an absolute among the aspiring and accomplished; a shared condition between the broken and the brave. The difference is in knowing how to set its energy into motion that carries you. Energy in motion. Emotion. A ready prompt for a journey, inner or outer, to discover your true north and live with clarity and purpose. That alone is enough to call yourself a great creator.

All the creative acts of art and life are heroic struggles. They are often shaped by untold failures and false starts before a suddenly cathartic release. With a great exhale, a new creation marks a new beginning sparked by an old struggle's end.

For the Love of Creation

A vision inspires action.

Creation is an act. Creation is an artifact. Creation is all of everything. Whatever you believe it to be, creation inspires living. I've made a life out of bringing creativity into the world however I can. It's a life I'm happy with and for which I feel a sense of purpose. It didn't come together the way I expected. I began as a musician, playing bass guitar professionally for the better part of two decades. Then I took a surprising turn and spent a decade building creative strategy teams for brands and businesses.

Music taught me to love the harmony of creation. Marketing taught me to believe in the value of creation. All the while, I'd been on an inner journey to reflect my outer one. Between Zendos, villages, and the back rooms of crystal shops, I sought answers to resolve the spiritual stirrings inside of me—and, with practice, inside of others. The mystical taught me to love the purpose of creation.

Despite my earnest enjoyment of each, these three identities of mine—a maker, a marketer, and a mystic—felt at times like embarrassments to each other. How could a maker sell out to brands, let alone a mystic? How could a marketer be so naïve as to put stock in the spiritual? I struggled with this. These enjoyments, as much space as they held for each other in my heart, were at war in my head. The anxiety was constant and rising. Then, I had the audacity to want to write a book. Another turn. A release prompting my pooled, stagnating anxiety to flow into a stream of creativity. First a trickle, then a torrent. The maker, the marketer, and the mystic within me were pushed into alignment by the common threat of this creative current. A self-apparent vision for the harmony and value of each became clear against the light of this new North Star: The mystic sees. The maker makes. The marketer shares. They all row together on the same river driven by and for the love of creation.

With little else than an inner commitment to create, experiences began to manifest before me in service to this purpose. As a mystic, I was asked to lead meditations for coworkers, to cleanse the energy of offices, and to provide tarot card readings to executives. As a marketer, I was asked to help businesses discover the meaning of their purpose. As a maker, I was asked to build teams designed to package actionable creativity. Soon, the skills I'd cultivated for each identity didn't just align, they served each other well. What is it to make and market something without a purpose? What is it to believe in something without harmony or value?

These aren't just questions. These are the tensions beneath the anxiety of our times. So often it feels like we're all aboard a rudderless ship of global culture, a place lacking a shared vision. We're not seeing the same North Star, and because of this we're imperiled by the collision of our conflicting journeys. Who has the facility to see a better story, to make it, and to share it? I don't know exactly, but I do know this: we can come together through the shared love of creation.

Our bodies may be small against the cosmic scale (we humans don't even take up the most biomass on our planet), but our spirits are infinite and our minds have the ability to follow the paths our spirits reveal to fill it across space and time. We have shown we can shape the earth in our image so convincingly we've become afraid of the consequences of our own power. The imaginations of our brightest luminaries in storytelling and science have plotted the means by which the candle of human life on this planet could spread like wildfire to the edges of the universe.

The visions are there. We have to make it. Whether or not we will is the everlasting question. This is what visions do. A vision puts the energy of anxiety into motion, propelled by the promise of purpose. Even this, the heaviest and most existential of human dreads, is moved by the power of creation. How might it move you, even if only just you, to retreat from the vision of curling up into nothing and instead reach for the vision of stretching out into everything?

As the Zen masters say, "Before enlightenment, chop wood, carry water. After enlightenment, chop wood, carry water." You are here. What are you going to do about it?

A Compass

The Seven Directions

A compass sets direction.

Emotions have a way of making themselves feel so big and making you feel so small. The sense of overwhelm is familiar, especially as it relates to the bad feelings. You cannot think your way out of a bad feeling. You can, however, feel your way through them. Therein lies the struggle of a tight focus on a "mental health" practice. It keeps you in your head, when the way out is often through your heart.

Anxiety is often the veil of a more complex emotion. It covers the nuance with the excitement of the unfamiliar. The moment you were born, your first exposure to the new sensations of air and light was overwhelming. So, you likely cried out in response to what felt at first like pain, but soon became familiar. Much of the disembodied anxiety you carry today is a less acute version of the same thing. Life is such a parade of new feelings entering your awareness, it's easy to spend all of it crying in some form. Inside the mind is an index of known words and memories by which familiar feelings can be explained. When a feeling is unfamiliar, though, it can't be fully explained. It can only be experienced. In the gap between the familiar and the non-familiar, anxiety guards the gate. It's easy to choose not to cross and find out how big or small your feelings really are.

This book offers a system of meditation and contemplation to help fill the gap. It's called the Seven Directions, and it functions like an inner compass to help you locate and size the feelings of your inner world and to read the energy signature of your emotions in order to help you discern the information they carry. It achieves this by segmenting your inner world into different directions of experience:

What is in front of you? (Front)

What is in your future? What are you moving toward? What do you give your attention to? What growth do you seek?

What is behind you? (Back)

What is in your past? What are you moving away from? What hides behind you in shadow? What healing do you seek?

What do you rest upon? (Beneath)

What is in the soil of your life? What is at your foundation? What seeds are planted and what roots grow in your land and in your body? What is your community? What is your ancestry?

What shines upon you? (Above)

What spotlight are you in? What activates you? How do you connect with the sacred? What inspires or guides you? Which channels do you hold open?

What do you receive? (Left)

What are the people, places, or things that influence you? What are you consuming? What stories are you taking in? What are the environments and sounds enveloping you?

What do you give? (Right)

How do you influence the people, places, and things around you? What is the effect of your presence? What stories are you telling? What are you manifesting? Where is your energy going?

What is in your heart? (Center)

What is at the intersection of all these other directions? What do you want to claim as your story? How do you connect with the unknown? What is your idea of authentic? What gives you a sense of both play and purpose?

Behind all feelings is awareness. Information that can guide you, if you let it. Observe your feelings and let them unfold before your watchful inner eye. When a feeling arises it can seem all-encompassing, hitting you everywhere at once. The Seven Directions empowers you to turn toward wherever that feeling is coming from and face it with the intention of fully understanding what the experience brings. From that understanding, you can decide what to do with it. You might find, as I have, that some of your deepest anxieties carry the most creative ideas indeed.

The Seven Directions as a framework for contemplation is great for spinning up an idea, turning it around, and seeing a clear path toward its creation. As a meditation, though, the Seven Directions becomes a compass for profound inner journeys. It is powered by how you breathe. What was the first thing that happened after you cried when you were born? You breathed . . . and then your journey began. If each direction of the compass points to a gate, then your breathing builds the bridges that cross through them.

Your breath is both a voluntary and an involuntary system. You spend most of your time not actively controlling it, let alone thinking about it. Your unconscious self is in charge. Yet, your conscious self can step in and take over. You have the ability to breathe however you choose to. How you breathe sets the rhythm of your being. Other involuntary systems like your heart rate, your digestion, your nervous system, even the hormones in your bloodstream that constellate your unconscious experience, are guided by how you breathe. The moment you take a conscious breath is the moment you initiate a dialogue with your unconscious self. When you breathe into each direction's feeling, who do you think is waiting for you on the other side of the gate?

How you breathe is how you move through your inner world. Every inhalation brings you closer to an attractive energy behind each gate (a feeling that draws you in). Every exhalation brings you closer to a repulsive energy (a feeling that pushes you away). The height of your inhale is the height of your gratitude. The depth of your exhale is the depth of your courage. Each of the seven directions is accompanied by a question designed to spark a conversation between your conscious and unconscious self. Your imagination, like your breath, is both a voluntary and an involuntary system. They can each be controlled by either your conscious self or your unconscious self and so act as a connection between the two. When you close your eyes, breathe consciously in a direction, and imagine a gateway unlocked by a question, you are opening a dialogue. A conversation begins between your head, the seat of your conscious intellect, and your heart, the seat of your unconscious intellect. They speak different languages, but they want the same thing: for you to live a rich and purposeful life. Their common language is within your imagination in the shared definition of sensation, color, and archetypal form. Symbols. Totems. Dreams.

The directions are channels formed by open questions meant to be filled by the creativity of your unconscious self, speaking in this common language of your imagination and mediated by the tempo of your breathing. The questions are open-ended because vagueness is favorable to unconscious expression. Each direction and corresponding question is meant to be interpreted in many different ways. As a channel, they are expansive enough to allow space for your creative expression, however it may speak.

It's a stunning experience the first time you ask something, and something other than your idea of "you" answers. That is your unconscious self whispering to you, passing on whatever whispers to it. This is the promise on the other side of the gate that the three-headed dog of your anxiety guards. Open the channels and let the creativity flow through. You'll be amazed at what you can do.

The Seven Directions is the compass of the creative process this book teaches. Each chapter offers an exploration of a different direction, reflected through the journeys that I've taken as a maker, a marketer, and a mystic.

With hope, my stories will inspire you to more courageously live yours.

At the start of each chapter you will find a symbolic rendering of each individual gateway meant to help you meditate or contemplate its meaning. Each gateway's illustration has been carefully constructed to capture the archetypal essence of its respective direction's question. All of them together complete the image of the compass that represents the Seven Directions as a total system. These images are abstract. If you wish, you can gaze upon these gateway images in an eyes-open meditation to affix your subconscious attention on the essential question each direction asks. If you can, imagine yourself drifting into them as you gaze. I encourage you to consider these illustrations as training wheels for the eyes-closed meditation in which you imagine each direction's gateway yourself as every chapter will guide. Eventually, you can construct your own idea of how each direction's gate is experienced in your inner world.

I understand that it's hard to grasp something designed to bypass the mind. To help, in the middle of each chapter, you will also see a diagram that represents more logically how the energy of the Seven Directions flows. Each diagram details the attractive and repulsive energies of each direction with all of them coming together to form the complete metaphysical compass of the Seven Directions. I've included these diagrams alongside every direction's gateway meditation so your mind can gain the satisfaction of knowing how it all fits together. It's a trick of meditation to keep the conscious mind busy with a chew toy like that so your subconscious heart can take control. The logical diagrams and the archetypal illustrations are designed to speak to both head and heart to help you more completely absorb each direction's teaching, whatever your intellectual lean. The full Seven Directions system diagram with each direction, energetic pole, and axis labeled is here for you below.

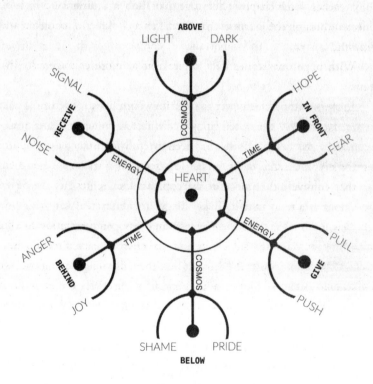

This is the compass of your inner world, within which your true north is up to you to decide. Align your inner world with the compass of the outer world and you can channel big creation into the world with a power beyond whatever canvas you might choose. The compass of the outer world points to north, south, east, and west. They each have their own rich history of character as imbued and discovered by generations of human culture. Much of the meaning ascribed to each is self-apparent in the nature of their direction. The sun rises in the east and sets in the west as the earth turns in that direction. For the peoples who settled on the lands north of the equator, the North is the home of cold and the South, the home of warmth. For those south of the equator, these associations are the opposite. Some traditions look toward the North Star for direction. Other traditions look toward the stars that rise with the sun in the east. Many traditions ascribe animals or totems to each direction to hold their meanings in symbol. The importance of connecting with the vitality of each cardinal direction's energy is universal to all cultures. Except for the modern one we've gotten lost in.

There is tremendous power in aligning yourself with one of the cardinal directions of the outer compass before engaging with the inner compass of the Seven Directions. It connects your inner world to the outer world and extends the bridge of your imagination out into reality. After cultivating the power to transmute anxieties into creations, you can decide where to take it. A key for you to consider: Art is subjective. Science is objective. The greatest creations come from those who know how to make the subjective and objective align. Each cascading layer of creative emotional energy in such an alignment connects and you become a channel for powerful, *powerful* things. When you cultivate creative energy in alignment with where you sit on the planet, you can tap into its collective story and find a place for your inner creativity within the outer needs of the world. You will find that at the center of it all is the stunning, calm stillness of nothing, but out of that center comes the wonder of everything.

A Star

The Zen Master's Cancer

A star lights the way.

We begin at the center, where we will meet again in the end. Sit with me at eighteen years old, cross-legged on a cushion atop a pinewood deck in central Massachusetts, outside the doors of a Japanese American Zendo to my left. To my right, a fiery sky announcing the day's sunset over a crisp glacial pond gently lapping at the shore beneath me. Seated in front of me, a man in his late sixties cloaked in a midnight black robe out of which emerged his shaven, aged head; more chiseled than wrinkled. The gaze from his left eye, twinkling. The gaze from his right, piercing. Long, wispy eyebrows crowning them both. He wasn't Japanese. He was an Irishman, who after decades as an outlaw LSD distributor, found himself as the recipient of a heavy dharma transmission from an embattled Japanese Rinzai Zen master who had brought the lineage to America. The transmission had made him the abbot of this order, and this was his monastery. It had taken a winding path, but this was how the energy of that lineage made its way to greet young me, a small-town suburban prince brimming with the sort of confidence that comes from walking through already opened doors.

I'd earned the privilege of sitting down for a one-on-one dialogue with this confusing Zen master in exchange for the other privilege of performing music for him and his monks. My musicianship was the basis of my abundant self-esteem, so I was up for the task. I'd been studying at a music school nearby and so was trusted to step into the dojo at the conclusion of their intensive weeklong silent meditation and sound out the first notes to help bridge them back to this plane where the rest of us play. My father, one of those monks in training, had disappeared to many of these retreats over the years and was eager for me to truly meet his teacher at this depth. I, a college student, was eager for the free meal I was told would follow.

"Who are you?" he asked me, cutting what had been a long silence after I'd settled onto my cushion.

"My name is Will," I replied, meeting the sharpness of his gaze.

Slowly, he shook his head. "*Who are you?*" His emphasis stretched across each word evenly.

Sensing that this wasn't going to be an easy conversation, I took a deep inhale with my nose and avoided his gaze as I sighed through my mouth. In the pause, I listened to the birds chirping in the trees behind me, and noticed the fiery sky peering through the branches. "I am a musician," I finally answered with a shrug.

"A musician." He nodded slowly. "What do you play?"

"Well, I prefer to write and play my own songs. I'm not very good at learning anybody else's."

"What do you write about?"

I paused again and felt a swell of nervousness rise from my belly and into my heart. "I, hmm. Well . . . I write about girls. You know, heartbreak and stuff."

"What's the point of that?" He laughed. I could see the Irish in the sudden flash of a glint of his eyes, betraying the stoic image of the monk in robes but adding to his spell, not breaking it.

Nervously, I mimicked his laughter. "I don't know, man. I write about that because it's, well, yeah, it's what I know."

"Do you?"

His question came like a pebble ricocheting off a windshield, just cracking the glass of my confidence with a snap that made me blink. I retreated a bit inside myself and thought. I knew that I knew lust. I *believed* that I knew love. I was afraid that I didn't truly know heartbreak. Or pain. I drew another breath, sat in the silence, and shifted my eyes to my hands. I looked with pride at the calluses on the tips of my fingers from years of practicing my instrument, but I could see that the rest of me was soft.

He cut the silence again, and leaning in sternly, he said flatly, "There is no point in creating art if it does not seek to express the truth." After pausing for a breath, he leaned back and asked me again, "*Who are you?*"

My eyes darted back to him, scanning the folds of his robes and the lines of age across his skin. I sensed something hard to grasp except to call it primordial or ancient flowing from him. It was this current of energy that rose from beneath his presence, this Zen lineage that had somehow come to him and was now sitting in front of me. Was the feeling coming from him? Or was it the questions? Maybe both? I didn't understand it, but it was enchanting. Taken as I was, I lost my hold on it when my mind flashed to the excitement with which my father would return home from his meditation retreats, recounting stories of his master's Zen riddles and the breakthroughs they'd led him to. A smile came over me as I remembered a riddle just like this. I felt I had cleverly snuck a peak at the answers to the test.

"I am . . . nothing," I proudly replied with a trickster's confidence.

With a slight raise of one eyebrow, his gaze shifted. The twinkle in his left eye grew into a flame. "You are nothing? Yet, *you* are here."

I felt like I'd been caught cheating. Or at the very least, the puzzle had deepened. I hadn't spied *these* answers to the quiz. My nervousness came back, rising now from my heart into my throat. I coughed out a laugh.

"Is there fear?" he asked me.

"Yes," I confessed.

"What is fear?"

"Fear is . . . it feels . . . I don't know."

"Fear." He smiled. "What are you afraid of?"

"I don't know. A lot of things. Getting sick and dying."

"Getting sick," he said. "Your dad told you I have cancer, yeah?"

I shook my head meekly. Unsure how to respond. Unsure how to feel.

"Have you ever felt cancer?"

My eyebrows shot up and my head jerked back. "No, I can't say that I have."

"Would you like to?"

A silence hung over us until he broke it and continued, "If you'd like, give me your hand." Slowly, with consideration, I placed my hand in his. He guided it up and gently laid my fingers upon his throat. "Right . . . about . . . there," he said. "You feel it?" Underneath the stubble of his neck, underneath the flesh of his aged Irish skin, underneath the steady rhythm of his heartbeat, I felt an even steadier, obstinate lump. Immovable. Firmly rooted in its place.

"Cancer. How interesting is that?" he exclaimed as his face lit up with an unexpected boyish excitement. "We'll see what happens next."

"You're . . . you're not scared?" I winced as I asked.

"Of course I am. But fear . . ." He smiled again. "What is behind fear?"

I thought about that boyish excitement I'd seen flash in his face a moment before. "Behind the fear . . . it feels like . . . I feel excitement."

"Good. Very good." His eyes looked at me piercingly again. His fist rose in front of his heart, and he grunted firmly like a warrior. Suddenly, he gasped, and his eyes opened wide as his hand shot up to block something unseen. Holding his palm toward me, he slowly began to turn it toward himself, his fingers quivering as they closed in as though he had caught something. His hand drifted toward his chest, and he drew a deep, deep breath as he held it to his heart. A tension. A dissipation. A release. His quivering movements made his presence feel inhuman yet deeply alive. It presented me with an image of naked existence that shook loose a disquieting emptiness in my own being into which I dropped. I felt my nervousness and my fear fall from where they had risen to my throat and down through my core into the center of the earth. I was pulled deeply into the silence within. He noticed. He saw. He nodded.

"The excitement of being aware. Being alive," he whispered. "Our order is called Rinzai Zen. It moves across cultures. It began in China before spreading to Japan and now here to America. It was practiced by the samurai. The way of the warrior. Eyes open. Aware, alert in every moment. Always alive because always ready for death."

"The way of the warrior," I parroted back quietly.

"There is fear. Behind that fear is excitement . . . and behind that excitement?" he asked, chin rising slowly.

"Awareness," I replied.

"Awareness." He nodded. "Awareness, and behind that, a deeper awareness of the awareness and again a deeper awareness of that until *you* are the stillness at the center transcending it all. Fear is just the turbulence around that center. Fear is the wind in your attachments. Fear in your identities. Fear in your dramas. It all swirls around like the weather. Melodramas are the storms and the tides on the surface wrapped around the stillness of the core." He found and locked onto my eyes. "What matters most is where you take your seat. Take your seat in the center, in the stillness, and see. *Who are you?*"

A long silence.

Finally: "I am nothing."

"Nothing is something," he quickly shot back.

"I am no . . . thing," I replied.

"I am?"

"No thing."

"No thing." He nodded. "Welcome."

Welcome. I've met you before in this place, where we will meet again in the end. No thing, out of which everything. This is the source of creative vision, whether as mystical as a dance's ecstatic movement or as mundane as a marketer's media plan. Who you truly are rests in the stillness of not being, yet that is the hardest place to find. Whether you identify as a maker, a marketer, or a mystic, finding the stillness of this nonexistence at your center will lead to *your* truth.

Remember. Why create art if it does not express the truth?

The way out is in.

This way is north.

Let us begin.

A Journey

Which Way Is North?

A journey brings experience.

Do you know which way is literally north? Right here. Right now. Which way is north? If you don't already know, take a moment to find it. Then ask, why? Why didn't you know? It's nothing worth feeling ashamed of, but it is something worth wondering. How was it that you've gotten so disconnected from something so simple? The animals know it. The plants know it. The machines know it. Yet most of us have forgotten it. You're not alone. We've all gotten lost together. Our separation from and journey back to nature is perhaps the defining journey of modern times. A vastly complex challenge revealed in the asking of one simple question. Which way is north?

Knowing the answer is one thing. Understanding it is another. The head knows; the heart understands. It's the difference between explanation and experience. Let's play with this. Let's take a journey. If you can, find a place to sit comfortably. Face the north. Once you do, focus your mind on what's in front of you, seeing as far as you can. With your eyes open, you may not see very far, but with your eyes closed, you can see through walls and past horizons. You know which way you are facing upon the earth, so let your mind travel north past the buildings, the forests, the mountains, and flowing bodies of water you know to be in front of you. Pass the frozen landscapes until you reach the pole at the top of the earth, home of ice and aurora. Close your eyes, and when you're done, come back here to this page. Go.

Now, take that same journey over the horizon behind you to the south. Then to the west on your left and then to the east on your right, all the way until by journeying across both, you find in your imagination the other side of this planet beneath you. Sit with that for a moment. Feel how this planet rotates, ever tilting you to the right as it spins to the east. You are here. Don't just *know* where you are; understand it. Feel it. Hold it as only you can.

You've located yourself; now breathe into it. Turn on the engine. Experience how much energy you can bring to this moment. Breathe out all of the air from your lungs. Hold steady with that emptiness, the uncomfortable lack of air, for a count of five . . . four . . . three . . . two . . . one.

Breathe in and relax. Did you feel the energy of that?

Were you agitated by a feeling of aversion to that experience? The depth of your exhale is the depth of courage. Holding yourself there is like drawing back and tightening the string on a bow. As the tension rises, soon nothing matters to you more than the desire for air. You want to get away from the energy of this experience and, like an arrow in flight, to feel the rush of air again passing through you again. There is courage in the discomfort. There is something creative in the anxiety.

Now, breathe in as much air into your lungs as you can. Fill all the way to the top and then some. Hold it in for a count of five . . . four . . . three . . . two . . . one. Breathe out and relax. Did you feel the energy of *that*? Did you feel how it was different? Instead of agitated, did you feel nourished by that experience? The height of your inhale is the height of your gratitude. Holding yourself there, you can almost feel how every cell in your body is drawing from its energy. It's like the wind sets every wheel of life spinning into motion within you. You find gratitude in the comfort. It's an energy you want to stay close to. Every new breath of air brings with it the creative promise of something new. See how good the uncertain can feel? Breathe out what you know. Breathe in what you don't. Wonder in between. The depth of your exhale is the depth of courage. The height of your inhale is the height of your gratitude.

This is the heart of human understanding you are endowed with. To know the directions of the inner and outer worlds you live in and to breathe the energy of your awareness into them. It's simple. It's powerful, but it often feels complicated. That's what this book is about. Getting from complicated back to simple again. Remembering what we once understood and have since hidden from ourselves behind the illusion of knowledge. As you progress through the journey of these pages, you will find that the basic elements of *direction* and *breath* are the only tools you really need to unlock the lessons. In learning to work with those two, you will strengthen your ability to work with the precious technology of being human . . . you will strengthen your ability to see not just what is, but what could be . . . and you will know how to make it. This altogether is the power of something I call *creative vision*. It is a gift we are all given, but it must be awakened. Creative vision is what you see with your eyes closed and is what colors you see with your eyes open. It is how you perceive the world when you are awake. It is the central narrator of your dreams. Creative vision is your story of who you are, where you come from, and where you're going. Wouldn't you like to be the author of that?

There Is No Eye in "See"

A lesson plants a seed.

The Seven Directions is anchored in meditation because meditation is like a gym where you can work to train your ability to be present in the moment. You'll find that creativity will just flow through you naturally with the strengthening from using this system, but don't hold onto the system itself too tightly. You don't have to drop into a meditation every time anyone asks you for a creative idea. The strength and the quickness will just be there. The meditation is the training. Life is the field of play. Creation is always here for you in the present moment. With good practice, you will be amazed at your ability to know what you need to know when you need to know it. You'll find yourself accessing ideas as though you were accessing an information server in the cloud. Where do these ideas come from?

A lot of systems of meditation are about getting away from your thoughts. They'll guide you with something along the lines of imagining yourself as the sky and your thoughts as passing clouds. Just let them drift away. I've practiced these kinds of meditations and received their benefits. That said . . . I think there are other ways to engage with our inner selves that are less difficult and just as, if not more, useful. What if you approached your inner world not as a sky you have to keep clear, but as a messy sandbox you can play in? What if instead of running away from your thoughts, you ran toward them? Grab them and ask them, "How did you get here?" That's the game I've been playing inside my head. It doesn't come from nothing, but it does come from Zen. Or, admittedly, an isolation of one of its principles I find particularly useful for cultivating creativity.

In mindfulness practices like Zen, there is this observation of "phenomenology"—the principle that what arises is to be apprehended as it is, in and of itself, without attachment. If you have an emotion like, say, fear, you would not observe it as "I am feeling fear." You would observe it as, "There is fear." There is no "I." No possessive self. There is only what arises. There is a thought. There is a feeling. There is a bug biting skin. I'll admit I'm still working on my unattachment to that last one, but that's the idea.

I've played with this idea of phenomenology in my meditation practice for a long while. It's a perfect example of how my identity as a mystic has served my identity as a maker and marketer. As my life has evolved into the career of being called a "capital C" professional Creative, I've found myself increasingly in high-pressure situations where I have to come up with a creative idea very quickly. Five minutes at a dinner table to convince some major brand's top executive why and how they should rethink their business, often with little to no preparation. On the other end of the spectrum, all-day brainstorm sessions with multiple teams across dozens of people packed into conference rooms with the expectation of walking out with a big idea. It was only a matter of time, bouncing between my meditation practice and these brainstorm sessions, that I would find a connection between the two. The phenomenology of an idea. Where creativity comes from.

First off, nobody *has* an idea. They just find it. If you want to walk that path of professional creativity and enter a brainstorming session effectively, don't come into it focused on sharing *your* idea. Focus on finding *the* idea. The most impactful and inspiring creative projects I've been a part of were all built on the foundation a self-apparent idea everybody at the table could see. If it's obvious, it's clever. A great Creative is like the Zen master who can catch a butterfly in their hand without looking and bring it gently toward their face unharmed for a closer examination. But you're not catching butterflies. You're catching ideas. I am not here to give you ideas. I am here to help you catch your own. Whatever path you may choose.

When I build and manage creative teams, I make a point of leading around this principle. A professional creative team's job in simple terms is to quickly come up with a lot of ideas that generate a lot of value. That is the "what" of any creative team. In the case of KarmaLab, the creative strategy team at Reddit, we described our "how" very succinctly in our mission statement: *to turn curiosity into understanding*. For us, curiosities were the butterflies we wanted to master catching in our hands. The big ones are exactly like the kind of unfamiliar feelings that give you anxiety, but these "curiosities" are aberrations in experience expressed in culture. This, at least for me, was also how our mission statement captured our "why." I've seen so many curiosities in culture and so little understanding. My hope is to do my part to help tip those scales into a better balance.

Seeking curiosities is not only about the individual, it's about the collective. Something that crosses your field of feeds and inspires you to ask, "How did you get here?" Oh, how I love catching curiosities and asking them questions. The first signs of new waves in culture like guerrilla gardeners who toss "seed bombs" of wildflowers into abandoned parking lots or digital communities who spent their time in pandemic lockdown trying to meet up on the astral plane. Quirky new hairstyles. Odd twists on fan fiction. The more out of place and weird and colorful they are, the more creativity they have to offer. The less you understand them at first, the better. Just like your thoughts and feelings.

Marketing is a wide field of play for creativity. It's where the other people are. Meditation is just you with yourself, but it is without a doubt the best place to exercise your skill in catching curiosities to discover what's bubbling up in culture to sharpen your instincts on catching the most exciting creative currents. When you enter your inner world, the thoughts that arise are a source of information. There are low energy thoughts among them, such as wondering what you should have for dinner. Mumblings of the mind. There are other thoughts that are very curious indeed. They tend to present vibrating with the high energy we experience as anxiety, charged with their own unique signature of attractive or repulsive frequencies. They are curiosities of your inner world surfacing with such an abundance of information that they kind of freak you out. Anxieties bring stories, some of which are worth telling. More of them than you may think are universally relatable too.

The Seven Directions system is offered first as a tool for focusing your attention in specific areas of your inner world. Then, it becomes a tool for focusing your attention on the outer world. That's a path to becoming a creative force able to find a common language between the depths of your unconscious self within you and the heights of culture around you. The creative gift is in the noticing. The more you tune in to what's inside and the more you check out what's around you, the more you begin to recognize common symbols that might flash in your visual field, or places held in memories that keep recurring, or songs that seem to play in your head. Even feelings in your body have a language you can discern with consistency of practice. They all correspond to the vast outer language of nature speaking to you at all times. *You* are not having the ideas. The ideas are happening in and of themselves. The only "I" in there is the awareness that is noticing creation in motion. Nothing at the center. Everything swirling around. The movement of feeling in between. That is creation in motion.

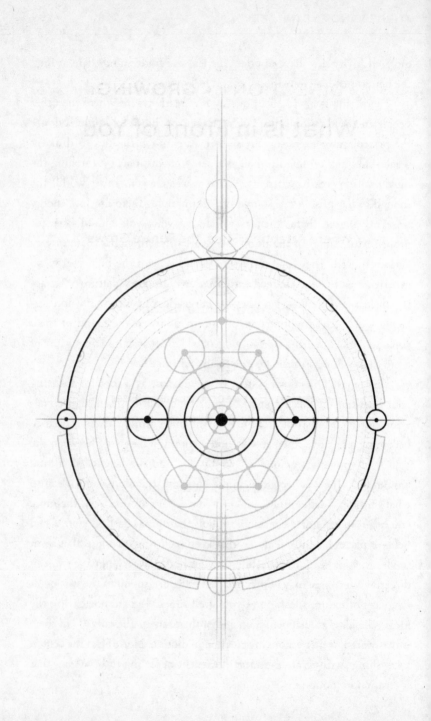

DIRECTION I ◆ **GROWING**

What Is in Front of You

Where Attention Goes, the Future Grows

The Art of Future Telling

Growing: Between Hope and Fear

The Oracles at Delphi

Creative Vision

Seeing Is Believing

A Point

Where Attention Goes, the Future Grows

A point starts somewhere.

Welcome. You are here. Drop your shoulders and relax. Roll out your neck. Drop your tongue from the roof of your mouth. Take a deep breath, count to seven, and exhale. Sit for a moment with a very simple question: *What is in front of you?*

What do you see?

Ever facing forward, what is in front of you is a bridge drawn by your eyes, upheld by the bond between what you see and what you believe. Open, your eyes greet a constant stream of information crossing that bridge in front of you in a steady parade of words, signs, images, faces, and colors. Every shape you see has a name. Every name has a story. Every story serves a purpose. In a world gone digital, the shapes we see and the stories they bring with them reach us from within the lights of glowing screens framed by an open world made easy to ignore. Media. Phones, tablets, televisions, computers, billboards. It's estimated that you receive somewhere between five and ten thousand media messages each day. All of them carry their own stories, serve their own purposes, wave their own banners of a promised future in the dancing parade before your open eyes.

Blink and you'll miss it, right?

Well, what if you *do* blink? What if you not only blink, but keep your eyes closed?

Your vision remains, but it turns inward and something magical happens. You stop being fed information and you start digesting it. Look no further than the scattershot three-ring circus of most of your dreams. A replay of the main figures in the day's parade, reconstituted into a new story's attempt to make it make sense. For many, what we see when we turn out the lights can be just as bright and chaotic as the world surrounding us. If I asked you to close your eyes now and look at what is in front of you in the waiting space of your imagination, what would you see? Try it.

What popped up in there for you? Here's a better question . . . how did it get there? And why?

A little blue bird flaps its wings as it lands back home in its nest. A raindrop splashes into the stillness of a morning pond, sending out ripples to its shores. Close your eyes for a moment again and come back. Did you see these images I'm putting in front of you with these words? Did you play out the stories they imply?

A beautiful lakefront house with an outdoor firepit and board game–ready dining table for that overdue family vacation. A stronger, sturdier off-road vehicle with room in the trunk for that mountain bike you've been meaning to get. A shadowy burglar lurking outside your window at night warded off by the new best-in-class home security system. The light of candles, the clink of glass, and the soft glide of silk on your skin. These are the sorts of stories you see a lot throughout the day that leave impressions in what you believe as you fall asleep at night. They aren't put in front of you for nothing. Someone paid money for them to be there for very specific reasons. The stories put on offer are made available to you at the price of your attention because where attention goes, the future grows.

Not just yours, but everyone's. The future is where fortunes live. To manifest a vision, it first has to be seen.

To be the maker of your stories and the deliverer of your dreams is a role as old as human culture. The vision keepers. It is to guide the current of manifestation that draws the line of human life between hope and fear into promised land. Promised by who and for what? The precious nectar of creative vision at the heart of people's beliefs and the power within it to shape what's in front of us has long been in the charge of the mystics whose priests, shamans, and medicine men were trusted to watch the bridge to our shared futures. Mistakes were made and much of that trust went missing. A different guild of human craft stepped in: Marketers. Merchants, masons, entertainers. *Innovators* of stories and dreams propelling a fixation on the future to get away from the failures of the past.

The impulse we call marketing that defines the globalized economy of attention we all share is built on the promise of keeping a bright future in sight. At the heart of the modern belief is the story that progress dreams. It's told in movie theaters. It's told on television screens. It scrolls across every digital feed. The more of us that pay attention, the stronger the shared belief in what to see. A higher vision of ourselves on the other side of the bridge in front of us that with focus, effort, attention, and resolve we might someday reach. What creative vision do you trust with your belief? How did it get there? Do you know where it will take you?

A Vision

The Art of Future Telling

A vision inspires action.

S o . . ." the man in front of me said and settled lackadaisically into the polyester of the Vegas casino couch. "What do you see?"

He relaxed with the body language of a man who finds comfort easily anywhere, and as he watched me, I massaged the back of my neck and held for a moment an expression on my face that could easily be mistaken for strain. I let out a sigh to let go of my long day with it.

I'd been cooped up in one of the top-floor suites with a wall of windows overlooking the Strip across a ten-hour run of show that had trains of marketing executives asking some version of this same question. What do you see? All of them, like myself, are members of a flock of somewhere around 150,000 marketers who make the annual migration to Las Vegas to talk about the future at the Consumer Electronics Show. That first week of January hits the media and marketing industries like an early morning alarm clock on a New Year's hangover. Jump out of bed, race to catch a plane, and dive into the flurry of handshakes that awaits.

The sun was getting ready to set over the desert mountains. I had no sense of how the air felt out there on the other side of that glass. Above the rattling bells and blinking lights of every casino floor, up through the oxygenated air vents and past perfumed hotel rooms are always about three to five floors of luxury suites. Who knows what happens in these rooms most of the year. For this first week of the year, those tower suites and the hallways in between become a beehive of bustling businesspeople power-walking through open hotel doors, brushing past the shoulders of each other's black or gray suits as their oversized trade show badges flap about on the lanyards around them. The air is heavily perfumed. It smells like sandalwood. No, it smells like jasmine. Actually, no, it smells more like pomelo. It depends on which room you're in, really. Whatever the smell, it is designed to engineer your feelings, wafting in on the distinct crisp of that oxygenated air that gets your blood pumping and your heart racing. Vegas. Marketing. Together. There's a rhythm to the whole machine, and it is fast, ambitious. It is meant to be, for that week, the hub of the wheel of fortune on which the spokes of the global markets spin.

I smiled at the executive across from me. My computer shared my exhaustion, humming louder than it should on the table behind me with a cable plugged into its side to project my prepared presentation onto the seventy-inch TV screen. In all capital letters on the screen read the title, "THE FUTURE IS ARRIVING," followed by a list of buzzy technology terms underneath. Blockchain. Facial Recognition. Self-Driving Cars. Cryptocurrency. Artificial Intelligence. 5G Technology. Machine Learning. Clean Energy. 3D Printing.

All of these were the topics I was prepared to describe the future of, choosing whichever depending on what kind of marketer stepped in. We'd had executives from nearly every kind of brand imaginable represented in our room over the course of that week. Brands that build the car you drive. The car you want to. The food you eat. The beer you drink. Your bank. Your computers. Your home. Your life. All of it. At least the parts of life you buy. All of them came curious about the same thing. What does the future hold? Where is the opportunity in it? Show us our fortune.

Sometimes in business jargon, you'll hear someone say "read the tea leaves" to talk about where markets are headed. That phrase tickles me because it's a bit literal for me. In my world, fortune-telling and trend forecasting, as marketers call it, are the same thing. The only difference is the costumes people prefer they're dressed in. I do both. Throughout my time working as a creative strategist, one who forecasts trends for marketers and comes up with ideas to play with them, I would also moonlight as a tarot card reader, taking appointments on nights and weekends. Despite jumping between crystal shops and conference rooms, I like to think I present mostly the same between them. My bag is always packed with tarot cards and a computer. I'm always absorbing the face in front of me, letting the inner world of their creative vision bleed into mine.

Reading tarot cards had helped me to cultivate a skill set at perceiving the connective stories in between people and things. Each of the seventy-eight meticulously illustrated cards in a tarot deck is densely packed with an extraordinary amount of information rich in symbols. Those cards, laid out on a table in equally meaningful arrangements, activate the aperture of trained creative vision. Our minds are, at a minimum, meaning-making machines. Put different arrangements of information in front of you, and you will start to see connections whether they are true or not. Therein lies the hidden step on the bridge many people trip on when they try to cross. Vision is not about seeing what's true; it is about seeing what's useful. Sometimes, vision is less about seeing what's there and more about seeing what's not—and therefore wants to be. That is the art of future telling. It's not a science.

Perhaps that's why marketers gather there for CES, a festival of the future where everyone convenes to talk about what's next. As a mecca for casinos and gambling, it's an appropriate setting for fortune-telling on the level of global industry and culture. Playing cards, the sort you see on casino blackjack and poker tables, are themselves an evolution from tarot cards. Four suits, numbered one through ten with their kings and queens. They used to be called "parlor cards" because that's where fortune tellers would deal them. Parlors, the forebearer of the casino, where wheels of fortune spin. As time went on, people threw away the meaning of the cards, but kept the parts of them useful for dealing fortunes and playing games with them. What a metaphor.

"What do I see? Yeah, you know. I'm seeing a lot." I started off this last future-telling session of this year's parade with some filler to stall for time. Self-aware of it, I shot him a smile. My friend across from me at that moment, I liked him a bit more than the other executives I'd been meeting with all week, to be honest. He had less pretense about any of it, which is the mark of someone who wields real power. He led marketing investments for a global brand you know. Our conversation would play a part in shaping his decisions on what the next year of that business would look like. Decisions that shift markets and change what millions of people do and do not get to see put in front of them. It was a conversation that would cast visions to shape stories for the masses to believe or buy. Some of culture's biggest changes start with a small conversation like this between two people. I will admit, those conversations are where I've always wanted to be. I knew from our past sit-downs that he didn't let presumption get in the way of a good conversation that might reveal something, hmm, useful. That's why we'd started meeting a few years ago after the parade, outside the pomp and circumstance of our company entourages meeting. No prepared pitch decks and rounds of executive intros. Just two people talking about what the other sees. I leaned forward in my seat and dropped into the list of that year's topics I knew business leaders wanted to hear from a creative strategist. "You've got everything AI and how self-driving cars will reshape cities and 5G—"

He cut me off right away. "Sure, but that's not interesting to me. Plenty of people are talking about those things already." He fired back. "What's *really* holding your attention?"

I broke eye contact and started to look around at the casino's abundant distractions. I saw people that dressed like me, walked like me, probably talked like me hustling from one meeting to the other with their conference badges tailing behind their necks, weaving through Vegas's blinking lights. I took a deep inhale of the oxygenated and perfumed climate-controlled air. It smelled like yuzu and patchouli. I looked to my right through the tinted-glass doors that muted the desert's bursting brightness on the other side. Back to my left, the false light of giant television screens with stock tickers, basketball games, and talking heads. A crowd laughed in the distance. A slot machine bell rang.

"Okay, fine." I fell back into my seat, letting my body language completely change. "But it's not what I would call good." My tone shifted. I stopped being the marketer and I started being the mystic. I left my head and entered my heart, and after a slow breath turned back to lock eyes with him. "This is all about to break." My hands gestured around. "I don't know how and I don't know when, but it has to happen soon. It just . . . has to. You know, I mean . . . this conference . . . this whole thing with tech. It's always been about *changing* the world. It's always been about innovating toward opportunity. I just feel this shift into not just innovating for thriving but innovating for . . . surviving. It's not the kind of thing an advertiser would want to hear or say. It's in the background, but nobody is really talking about it out front. We don't want to, but it's there. I don't know how to explain it, but I sense it in everyone. It's absurd, right? We're here making decisions about what people focus on and there's something *everybody* is feeling but none of us are talking about it."

I stopped for a beat and then continued, shaking my head with my eyebrows drawn down in self-conscious concern. This was an odd thing for me to talk about with this person. It felt like going off script. I was supposed to give fortunes, not talk about doom. Nothing in what I was saying was good for business. "Something is coming. I don't know what it is, but *something* is coming." I started shaking my head. My heart was pounding. "I don't see an endless horizon like I used to. I see a cliff.

Yeah, there's the climate and everything, but that story always feels far off and slow moving. Something wants to happen in the immediate like an emergency brake being pulled. I don't really expect this to make any sense, but there's a word that just keeps coming up for me, rattling around in my head, and . . . and I can't explain why and I don't entirely know what it means." I winced at my own embarrassment, no longer masking anything, and shrugged as I said it. "Heal. The word is *heal*. Right? We look at the future and we want to change it, but what about healing it?"

He let out a long sigh and rubbed his hand over his forehead, looking earnestly exhausted. "Yeahhh." His voice whispered roughly in a sigh, his hand dropping back to his lap.

The embarrassment in me swelled. It was too much. Corny. Idealistic. Naïve. Indulgent. A believer, not a broker. Someone in my position is not supposed to be so idealistic and speak from the heart like that. We're supposed to be sober, measured, and have the mental discipline to look at culture's tides and not get taken by its currents. I braced for whatever would come next.

He looked up and locked his gaze onto me again. "That's what it is, isn't it?" His face had gone soft. He could see it too. There was a deep mournfulness in his eyes. A long silence held us in a human moment, a moment rich in meaning borne from an arrangement of things that will never be repeated again. "The real question is, what are we going to do about it?"

That was January of 2020. Only weeks later, global markets screeched to a halt and the planet fell into the silence of a global pandemic lockdown that would last the better part of two years. The virus had spread rapidly through the interconnected systems of conferences and travel and trade, shutting all of it down suddenly. Market squares everywhere emptied. The lights and sounds of casinos and stadiums turned off mid-game as people were told to go home. It hit like a thunderbolt, stopping every parade crossing every bridge to every future. We all had our plans and it all had to change as everything and everyone dropped into the free fall of society together not knowing when or where or if we'd hit bottom. The game stopped. The world had indeed changed . . . and it was our economic ambitions that changed it. The only thing for us to do was to heal.

Heal was indeed the word, the right fortune to capture a vision for what was in front of us. It was a guidepost that revealed the path ahead, but not how to take it. Anyone who was paying attention saw it in their own way. When the shock of 2020 arrived, the vision became a reality and we all had to define for ourselves what it means to heal, as individuals and as a collective. In the rebuilding that followed, an evolving focus on health and wellness catapulted a new paradigm of healing to the forefront of cultural attention. There were those who got busy focusing on what was true, and there were those who got busy focusing on what was useful. Fortunes were made . . . and lost.

Beyond the growth of global wellness to a $4 trillion industry, beyond the billions of dollars in increased revenue made by pharmaceutical companies that took a war footing against the virus, shifting perceptions of mental, social, and political healing transformed the stated values of nearly every industry and community. A tidal wave of change hit fast, thinning the herd of those of us who would make the annual migration to Vegas. Fifty thousand advertising jobs and tens of billions of dollars were lost in 2020. In the following years, more than two hundred thousand jobs were lost at tech platforms among seismic shifts. Trust in established brands and marketers fell to an all-time low. Surveying almost four hundred thousand people worldwide, the global advertising agency Havas Media expressed shock when they found that 71 percent of people were not convinced brands would deliver on their promises and that 75 percent of people wouldn't care if a brand disappeared overnight. Less than half of the people surveyed saw brands as trustworthy. Meanwhile, the entertainment industry tanked, falling from $42 billion in revenue to $12 billion in 2020. Trust in who takes the role of vision keeper was changing again. People stopped paying attention. Or, at the very least, where people spent their attention began to move. The world's need for stories never fades, but who it wants to write them can and will change.

As the media and marketing industry reeled, voices emerged from the crowds outside industry's gates to champion their visions for what the world needs, rising in response to the hopes and the fears in front of everyone. Audiences swarmed quickly around these new voices, growing feverish, cultish, restless, and often at odds with each other. Mainstream culture was fracturing. Offering explanations carrying a sense of certainty, speaking to the world through the window of digital screens from the isolation of their homes, this newly empowered wave of vision keepers built digital media channels and commerce platforms to establish small empires. Brandishing titles like content creator or influencer, the "creator economy" was born. By the end of 2022, at least two hundred million content creators speaking to an audience of over four billion social media users established a $100 billion market with educators, coaches, and writers representing a majority. Within that, meditation and mindfulness ballooned to become its own multibillion-dollar industry as people around the planet searched for answers grappling with what the World Health Organization cited as a 25 percent increase in anxiety and depression triggered by the pandemic of 2020.

Makers acting as marketers, playing the role of mystics. The world has a way of turning upside down. The new becomes old and the old becomes new again, while the world just keeps on turning. In a deck of tarot, there is a card called "The Wheel of Fortune." It reveals that fortune is always in motion. As a fact of life, there are times when you are up and times when you are down. Growth is in how you roll with it. Changes happen quick. Healing happens slow. Look in front of you. What do you see?

A Compass

Growing: Between Hope and Fear

A compass sets direction.

Why not be your own vision keeper? In the future, the story that's coming can't change, but the facts can still be written. In the past, the facts of what happened are written, but the story that tells it can change. What is in front of you is the direction that brings you growth, as determined by where your attention goes and how you move into the future. Grow strategically, and you find fortune. That is life. That is love. That is business. That is the human experience of passing through time as individuals and as collectives.

To cultivate creative vision for what's in front of you, you are taking conscious control of where you send your attention, and thus how your future grows.

There are two energetic poles for you to journey between as you place your attention forward. An attractive energy and a repulsive energy. Your negotiation between these two makes for your guidance system. The

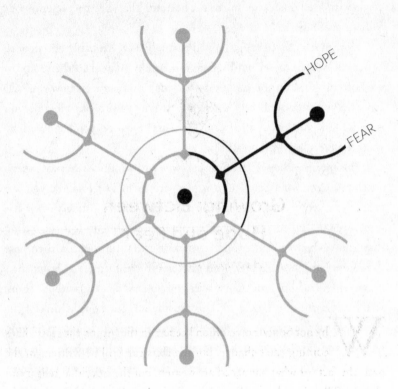

attractive energy in front of you is *hope*. Your aspirations. Hoping your dreams will come true.

The repulsive energy in front of you is *fear*. Your concerns. Fearing your nightmares will come true.

Generally speaking, neither will come true. That's the funny thing about visions being more useful than true. You don't see precisely what will happen, but you do see what will guide you. Follow the guidance with your breath. With every inhale, your attention drifts closer to your hopes. With every exhale, your attention drifts closer to your fears. Notice the character of the thoughts that arise in each phase as you sway in between. Take a moment to be with that. Imagine a meter, and breathe in as much as you can, seeing that meter rise to the top. Now breathe out as much as you can and see that meter fall to the bottom. That meter represents your full range of breath.

How much of that range do you normally use? Probably not all of it. Where do you find yourself breathing normally? Closer to the top or to the bottom? How do you suppose where you breathe affects how you feel? How do you suppose how you feel affects how you think? How do you suppose how you think affects how you act? How do you suppose how you act affects how you breathe?

The energy of hopes and fears can *both* easily induce what we experience as anxiety. They bring an urgency with them to *act now* so you can properly set your course toward or away from them. Anxiety itself has often been described as a kind of temporal displacement. It is the feeling that arises when your attention is stuck in the future, rather than here in the present moment. Well, you can't get to the future any faster than it's arriving. Imagine time like a river and you are floating with it. Think of the left bank of the river as the shoreline of your hope. Think of the right bank of the river as the shoreline of your fear. As you keep floating on with the current of time's river, the most control you have is in how you drift toward one bank or the other. Take a few breaths with your eyes closed playing with this visualization. Every inhale drifting you closer to your hopes and all that greets you on its shores. Every exhale drifting you closer to your fears and all that sneers on its shores. Back and forth with every breath, lilting gently in between without ever reaching either. Close your eyes and go in. Come back when you're ready. What did you see? Take note of the details.

Between those riverbanks, maybe, when you visualize what's in front of you, you see some rapids coming farther downstream or something that gives you anxiety along an approaching shore—this is like seeing a big story that's coming. You'll want to place yourself in the right spot between the river's banks to take the ride into that story however you please. Where attention goes, energy flows and so grows your future. What you hold in front of you in your creative vision guides the future you manifest. You have the ability to see what you can grow toward. Why not use it?

It's not just about avoiding your fears. Rapids can come on both sides. Realizing your hopes can be just as intense of a ride as realizing your fears. Both can also be surprisingly smooth. Any major life transformation is a great example. Graduating school. Getting married. Starting a family. Those can be the realization of your hopes but can for sure create some rough rapids. When you're looking ahead at life's passages like those, the story is coming one way or the other. That much is certain. It's the facts that tell it that are up for change. The who, what, where, and when. You can take it easy or you can look for a thrill. Just don't make the mistake of thinking your hopes will always be easy and your fears will always be a thrill. Sometimes, you can't escape the rapids and you've just got to ride it through. My greatest growth has come from navigating the roughest rapids.

Let's spend a little time in this.

I'd like to share with you a meditation to help you explore this direction as deeply as you would like, whenever you would like. Take as much time with it as you need. Revisit or reuse this as much as you need. In this meditation, you will open a gateway to your unconscious and initiate a dialogue that allows your deeper self to answer a question you will consciously ask: "What is in front of me?" Your unconscious is a powerful ally in life's journey. It wants to help. It is you, after all.

To bridge a conversation between your conscious and unconscious self, they need a shared language. This is, at their core, what a lot of the old mystical systems like tarot are built to provide. A shared language between creative visions and inner worlds. Your shared language between these parts of yourself can be anything. That's the point of asking a question like "what is in front of me?" It creates an opportunity to establish signs or memories or words or experiences within the creative vision you see when you close your eyes that will become the alphabet of this language. It begins with the gateway. This is the gateway that will bring you into the open field of your imagination *in front of you*—the inner landscape of your hopes and fears. What should that gateway look like? It's up to you. But, to help, you can find an illustration of a gateway at the start of this chapter. Artfully rendered with archetypal meaning in mind, it's made to speak to your heart. Gaze upon it for a while. Contemplate it. Internalize it. Then use a version of that as a starting point for the meditation.

Finally, get comfortable. You can be seated on the ground cross-legged with a cushion or not. You can be seated in a chair with your feet flat on the ground. Being seated upright rather than lying down is important for this meditation because of its play with the directions. If that's not possible, do your best to lie upright, if you can. Take a few moments to roll out your neck and limber out your spine with some stretches. I like to bow my spine back and forth and side to side to clear some space in there. The feeling I look for is for my spine to be like a snake rising out of my hips like they're the basket of a charmer. Chin slightly tucked, crown of the head tall to the sky. Dignified. Like a king or queen seated upon their throne. Not a bad way to feel. When you've found what's right for you, go ahead and begin the meditation.

One last thing . . . do you know which way is north? Find it and face it.

◆ MEDITATION EXERCISE ◆

Take three slow breaths, holding at the top and bottom for as long as you'd like. Every inhale in through your nose. Every exhale out through your mouth. Listen to the sounds that surround you and fall into presence with the movement, however it meets you.

*When you are ready, close your eyes and breathe in, imagining light from above dropping into your heart, and then with your exhale, breathe out that light **in front of you**. Only about six feet. See the space. Notice what is there when you imagine it and what is not. Close your eyes, go in, and come back when you're ready.*

On your next breath, see in your imagination beyond whatever walls hold you. Breathing in light from above into your heart and then breathing it out in that direction, all the way out to the horizon as far as your creative vision can see. Close your eyes, go in, and come back when you're ready.

On your next breath, see past the horizon. See in your imagination the opening of a gateway. The gateway appears or feels however you want it to. Beyond this gate are the answers to the question "What is in front of you?" Once you go in, take your time and breathe through as many cycles as you want to. Every inhale drifts you toward the energy of your hopes. Every exhale drifts you toward the energy of your fears. Remember, the height of your inhale is the height of your gratitude. The depth of your exhale is the depth of your courage. Explore.

Notice the thoughts, feelings, and experiences that arise in response to that question. What is in front of you? Everything that arises is information. Everything that arises is useful. Look, listen, and feel. Vision comes in all forms. There are no coincidences when you ask the question and move through the gate. Take your time and experience them. If it feels like nothing is happening, you can always breathe out and ask the question again and breathe in to see what replies. When you are ready, close your eyes and go in. What is in front of you? Come back when you are ready. ◆

When you have gotten comfortable with this meditation, do it on your own without guidance. If meditation is not your thing, consider using this as a contemplation exercise. With either practice, this becomes an intuitive compass that will help guide your creative thinking and expression . . . not just vision. You can use it for a general check-in or you can focus it on a specific project you are working on. With a journal, write down whatever thoughts arise when you ask yourself the same question. *What is in front of me? What are my hopes and fears?* Whatever answers, however it does . . . is both true and useful for you. You are your own vision keeper.

A Star

The Oracles at Delphi

A star lights the way.

The roads we walk to our future are paved over the trails of our past. Hard concrete over soft soil, but the lines they draw are the same, even if we forget they are there. My job as a creative strategist is like a paved highway over the dusty trail of a much older vocation. It takes me places quickly. It's easier to speed ahead toward the next destination than to idly contemplate the scenery passing by. Every now and then, though, the colorful flash of some curiosity will catch your eye. Look at it closer and it'll teach you something about the road you travel on.

In 2019, I was on an airplane every week traveling to a new city with a new conference. Each city held a different stage where I could share the same story, a vision for the future I had shaped with my employer, Reddit. At the very end of the year, I'd been sent out to a small but mighty marketing conference in Athens, Greece, where heads of brands and advertising agencies gathered in the nearby Mediterranean beach sands of Marathon to confer about the future. It was a symbolic choice because while Marathon is a small town, it holds a big story. One that connects history and marketing. It is the ancient battle site from which a battle-worn soldier had famously run the twenty-six-mile road back to Athens only to collapse on the steps of the republic uttering a single word, "Nike!" The name of the Greek goddess of victory. It meant that the Greeks had stood their ground against an invading force to halt a devastating war. It meant the survival of their entire civilization. The power of that story has continued to run for thousands of years into today beyond just the shores of Greece, riding along every sneaker brandishing a swoosh to represent the dominant global sports brand and their famous mantra: *Just Do It*. Yesterday's goddess of victory lives on in a multibillion-dollar apparel brand today.

Worthy ground for marketers to gather upon, indeed. What followed was a few days and long nights of revelation and revelry. Discussion about the future of the industry and the latest turns in the global economy. The opportunities and responsibilities for our brands. Coming together over food and drink and making plans like that cliff of change in 2020 wasn't coming. On the last night, a small offshoot approached me with an invitation as I leaned over the bar watching the dance floor in front of me. They'd heard of a place called Delphi that supposedly had some beautiful ruins up in the stunning views of Mount Parnassus, just a couple of hours' drive away. They were thinking about getting away and renting a van the following day. Was I interested? "Sure." I finished my drink and laughed. "Count me in." Not a month earlier, I was out to dinner with a brilliant friend who had gushed to me about his enchanting trip to Delphi. I'd never heard of it. The morning after that dinner, I received the last-minute invitation to take a colleague's place at this conference in Greece. Something mystical, it seemed, was calling. I long ago learned to say yes and follow those signs.

Nursing a headache, the journey began with an early morning drive up to the mountains farther inland. A man named Leonidas, our driver and guide, gave us a history lesson on the way. For thousands of years, Delphi was forgotten. Buried under the dirt and faded into myth. Whether it ever really existed at all became a question. Then, one day at the dawn of the twentieth century, deep in the mountains northeast of the bustling capital of Athens, Greece, the daylight found Delphi again.

The air is crisp and the light peculiar up there at the altitude of Delphi's summit. It's brighter. At midday, it's tough to look directly at the marble ruins with all the light they reflect. You have to squint to really see them. When you do, rainbows appear in your eyelashes at the corners of your vision. The ruins themselves rest in front of a towering limestone cliff. When a bird chirps, or a rock tumbles, the sound of it will reflect as brightly off its walls as the sun does off the marble ruins. Everything is showered with the presence of light and sound on high. It's a beautiful place, yes. That's for sure. The scenery adds life and luster to the mysterious stories that people have long told about the place. They say a god lives up there. When you see those rainbows and hear those echoing sounds, it feels true.

That god's name is Apollo. Like a constellation of ideas held within a brand, Apollo is the Greek god of light, music, harmony, medicine, and prophecy. It's said that it was his presence that stewarded the development of Greek civilization and brought its highest inventions and culture into being. Enormous visions like the idea of a system for justice and the idea of keeping records of history. Institutions whose existence we take for granted now, but at some time had to be born. Apollo, also being attributed as the god of music and of prophecy, certainly piqued my interest as a strange line to draw. I was eager to learn what could be the relationship between those two.

What happened at Delphi? It all began when a crack split open in the earth. We don't know when the vapors started to emerge, but we do know it was somewhere around 1600 BCE when a goat herder named Coretas watched his flock stir into a frenzy for no apparent reason. When he climbed his way closer to help comfort the crying and leaping animals tumbling down the hillside, he felt himself ecstatically transported to another realm that he'd later describe as "outside of time."

He raced back to town and shared his story with the others. He swore to them he had seen visions. He foretold future events. They doubted him but when those events he spoke of came to pass, word spread fast and the frenzy spread with it. Visitors from all over came to see the crack in the earth, to experience for themselves how it feels to be thrown outside of time.

Sadly, some people fell into such a fit that they threw themselves into the crack, falling deep into the mountain. That created problems for the villagers nearby so they roped it off and built a shrine. They said the site was too sacred, too powerful, for anyone to just walk into. Reasonable and fair, really. Still, their curiosity about what the vapors could do persisted. It turned out that the women of the village could hold their own with the power of the vapors best. So began the order of the priestesses of Apollo who were elected to speak his prophecies that appeared to them as visions in the fumes. The oracles. Always three. No more, no less. Why? Their station was to sit on a three-legged stool over that crack in the earth, breathe in the vapors, and share the visions . . . for hours at a time and for thousands of visitors.

Eventually, the shrine grew into an entire temple complex dedicated to Apollo. People came from all over the ancient world of Greece. They would wait in a line snaking all the way down the mountain for their chance to step across the breach onto Apollo's sacred grounds and ask a question of the oracles waiting in the stillness of the sanctum.

As the visions of the oracles brought more fortune to more folk, it became the fixation of Greek's wealthiest kings. As the oracles brought them fortunes, the temple became overrun with their gifts of gold and statues. Delphi's reputation grew, and the line down the mountain grew with it. Soon, the line was crowded with merchants selling wares to the waiting seekers, anything that could be given as tribute to the oracles in hopes of a better prophecy. As people from all corners of the world began gathering at Delphi, they would etch their names and news from their homes into the marble stones lining the path to the temple complex so their stories could sit among the treasures of kings and nations otherwise long forgotten. It was a birthplace of historical record. The front page of the ancient world. In this way, even without a visit to the oracle's sanctum, simply passing through Delphi became a way to confer. This only amplified the bustle around it, which itself became its own draw. Before long, there came to be massive festivals hosted outside the temple's walls. A theater. A racetrack. Delphi became a pilgrimage for mystics, merchants, gamblers, and politicians alike. It was a Las Vegas, Vatican City, United Nations, and Louvre Museum combined. A playground for the profound and the profane where hopes and fears are brought to fruition and fortunes are made in between.

Thousands of years later, when I arrived at its ruins, I drank from the still flowing spring. I walked up the steep slope of the mountain past the place where a grand tower of snakes winding around one another that held Delphi's flame once stood. The vast complex of temples and festivals today looks like not much more than a rock quarry. Hard stone crumbling back to soil. I marveled at the etchings of ancient stories that still remain visible. It was like seeing in stone the same human behavior that people today look for as they scroll across their screens searching for answers. Same vision, different time. Old path, new road.

I considered the three phrases that were once written on the arch entryway of Delphi when it still stood, artfully chiseled high above the bustling line in large, emboldened letters for all who passed through to see. If they were to take nothing away from their visit, they were to take away these guiding principles:

Know Thyself.
Nothing in Excess.
Surety Brings Ruin.

The oracles at Delphi shared visions that shaped the strategies that perpetuated Greek civilization from total ruin through a sequence of prophecies that confounded kings. The curious words of the oracles would all come to pass into the certainty of history, whether people understood them when they first heard them or not. The cryptic words of intuition sound weird when describing the future, but obvious when describing the past. It seemed the oracles at Delphi had perfected the art of future telling. *Pray to the winds*, they said ahead of storms that sank enemy fleets. *Safety in walls of wood*, they advised ahead of decisive victories within wooden ships. *A great empire will fall*, they warned a king who mistook it as a promise for his empire's victory all the way to its ruin. *The city or the king will be torn limb from limb*, they warned the famous Spartan king Leonidas before he and his three hundred sacrificed themselves in battle to save their city. Visions held in words offer no hard truths, only the soft hints of guidance.

At the center of an entire civilization's rise and fall, fortune and ruin, is the deep stillness of an inner sanctum where fortunes were given. It's an odd thing, I thought as I sat among its fallen temple, that vision, once at the beating heart of how civilization is created, somehow fell into embarrassment on the journey from ancient to modern along with the other vocations that surrounded it. The Greek model for civilization set the trails on which we've built modern roads. The politician, the athlete, the banker, the academic, the entertainer, the healer. All of these vocations are held aloft in modern culture's embrace. What happened to the oracles? They had been so central, so essential, to the formation of empires and then faded into the obscurity of silly superstition.

I sat back against the time-weathered stones in the crisp mountain air of Delphi's modern day and thought about the whispers of the past that speak of ways to see the future. I hadn't meant to be there. I hadn't meant to take any of the roads that brought me to this place. Not the job that had found me, nor the invitation that had brought me to Greece. I had only been following my visions, walking the line between my hopes and my fears to trying to make something of what I can do. Toying with some of the ground's limestone pebbles in my hand, I turned my gaze over to the only still-standing building of the whole temple complex. The proudly polished pillars of the Athenian treasury just steps downhill from the crumbled oracle's sanctum. The house of fortune, the only part of the whole place fully salvaged from ruins. I stepped up to a plaque and read its story. It was dedicated to Delphi to house the spoils of Athens's victory at the Battle of Marathon. Nike, indeed. I stood up, dusted myself off, and walked back to join the marketers, smiling with a new vision Mount Parnassus had given. Maybe when the dirt was wiped off Delphi only a few decades ago, the story, the vision, the dream of the oracles stepped into the light again.

A Journey

Creative Vision

A journey brings experience.

L et's explore this idea of vision a layer deeper.

There is the vision you see with your eyes open and the vision you see with your eyes closed. Creative vision is about what you see without your eyes whether they're open or closed. It is the programming code of your experience, determining what you notice and what you don't, both in the dark of your imagination and in the light of your surroundings.

The human mind is a meaning-making machine. It looks for pattern and connection in whatever is put in front of it in order to make sense of things. Where order doesn't exist, your mind will make it up. Perception is selection. Every moment puts a limitless amount of information in front of you, yet there is a limit to how much you can perceive. That you make choices about what you see is unavoidable. To be conscious of those choices is to claim your vision as a force of creation; to take your seat on a higher throne of human involvement in nature; to be more than just a consumer of it, but a creator.

This is the skill of artists and oracles, inventors, luminaries and strategists, those we call "visionaries" who not only see the future but create it. While it's exciting for some to imagine the way of visionaries to be out of reach, I find it more exciting to realize it's well within your grasp. Vision is a skill that can be trained like any other. Cultivate it and see the mystical become mundane and the mundane become mystical. Life becomes your canvas, because it always was. You can stare at it blankly, or you can start playing with the paint. Becoming visionary starts with taking charge of what you see.

Begin the journey with your eyes open. What do you see? Look up and take notice of what you notice. Notice the objects in front of you. Notice the spaces in between and the distances behind. Take a breath and relax into the light, the color, and the movement of all that you see. Just perceive it. Now, take notice of the stories that ride upon each detail of what you see. Observe the meaning-making machine of your mind in action as it conjures stories of what's in front of you, where it comes from, and where it's going. Notice the ideas of ownership, of purpose, of quality that color everything in your vision.

Lock in one object in particular. Choose any you'd like. As I write these words, I can see a door across from me. I can see that it is brown and shaped like a tall rectangle. It is built of wood inlaid with cuts that I would describe as cottagey, matching the color and style of the room it belongs to. I remember it opens inward, and what I can see of its hinges support this idea; however, I haven't tried opening it the other way. Maybe the hinges are double sided. Past that, I only have a general idea of what's on the other side of the door. I can't see.

This marks the edge where observable sight ends and creative vision begins. The mind models what it doesn't actually see. We don't actually know what's on the other side of our doors, but our minds generate a useful vision. That doesn't make it true. Even many of the facts of observation are, at the core, useful fictions. That the rectangle of wood is something called a door isn't a base level fact; it's a useful fiction. It's a story as subjective as the notion of what "cottagey" means to me versus what it means to you. Look at that object in front of you and give this a try. Find the edge of your creative vision.

The world you see with your eyes open is colored by assumptions that help you navigate the world quicker, even when they're wrong. It's easier to take for granted that a door is a door when your objective is to walk through it. The visionary, however, knows how and when to rethink these assumptions. They've opened their eyes twice and seen that on the other side of a world covered with assumptions is a world open for creation. If you've been programmed to think like a consumer, then you assume everything has already been made. A door is a door. It's made to be opened or closed, sometimes locked. That's it. If you've been programmed to think like a creator, then you assume everything is yours to make of it what you will. I've seen doors turned into canvases, snow sleds, firewood, and coffee tables, among other things. New creations that didn't exist behind the veil of the assumption that things are already made. Open your eyes, then open them again. Be creative with your vision. What do you see in front of you?

Let's go another layer deeper. Eyes closed, your vision works the same. It just removes sight from the picture. You are left only with your modeling of the world, the framework of assumptions on which your experiences are built. Thoughts, images, memories, even colors and shapes flash in your vision when your eyes are closed. Many of these are like contrails left in the sky of your imagination by the flights of media you consume. Stories that capture your attention with drama, intrigue, urgency, with a signature sense of something unresolved, cloud the weather of your inner world with left-behind assumptions that, unchecked, will mount into a feeling of disembodied anxiety. Is that anxiety yours? Or an algorithm's? The spiritual smog can be dissolved with the penetrating eye of creative vision. Claim your vision. Contemplate what you see, inside or out. Notice what you notice and break down the assumptions of what you see. Find a base level of "not knowing" and you'll find you can rethink and rebuild your inner world, then outer, from there.

Let's go another layer deeper yet again. Throughout this book, each chapter's compass meditation of the Seven Directions asks you to use your imagination to "see" a gateway and contemplate what it holds on the other side. This is a functional fiction to help you co-create with the mystery of life through the translator of your unconscious. Just like a door is a functional fiction for a journey in the outer world, a gateway is a functional fiction for a journey in the inner. That is why each chapter begins with an illustration of a gateway designed for your interpretation of its detail's meaning. They serve as a helpful aid to kick-start your own creative vision of what a gateway should be.

In these meditations, your vision of those gateways serves as a conduit to the great mystery of "not knowing," the "no thing" where the pure creative potential of the unconscious realm resides. These gateways work something like a black hole. A swirling portal of energy with an event horizon past which you cannot see. The metaphor of the black hole is apt. For one, because they represent perfectly what it's like to stare into the edge of what we know. Everything past a black hole's event horizon is a mystery. The same can be said about staring upon a gateway to the unknown in your imagination. It's also an apt metaphor because the eyes of science have long only envisioned black holes in theoretical physics, a form of creative vision, until recently, when the first actual image of one was captured. We can now literally see black holes as they are. Unfathomably dense gravity wells surrounded by vast glowing disks of burning matter, some of them bookended by high-powered jets shooting energy back into the cosmos around them at near light speed. What an image. These aren't just empty wells with a void at the bottom that twists and tangles the laws of space and time. They are, paradoxically, also fountains. Stuff goes in, energy comes out. For the gateways, story goes in and feeling comes out. Instead of moving matter, they move meaning.

Let's go one more layer deep and experience this as a journey.

In contemplating these gateways, the focused attention of your creative vision works like an engine riding along a current running between your head and your heart to open the gateway to mystery. Your heart holds feelings. Your head holds thoughts. Thoughts and feelings are the space and time of your inner world. The marriage between them births energy and form. Fusing them together with the light of your attention, you produce a gateway as powerful as a black hole. A portal you can journey into for visions.

Three points to a triangle. Your heart, your head, your gateway. Holding your feelings, your thoughts, your visions. The functions of the maker, the marketer, the mystic. All of these work together to power the engine of your creative vision to shape how you experience your inner and outer worlds. A question is the key that turns the engine on. The thought of a question arises in your head. *What is in front of me?* Your attention moves it to your gateway to become a vision. *What do I see?* Your attention moves it to your heart to become a feeling. *How do I feel? Is there hope? Is there fear?* Your attention moves it to your head to answer with a thought, which becomes another question. *Why?* A cycle of breath with every question that keeps it moving. The cycle continues. With every cycle, a clearer and bigger story.

Get comfortable and settle in to a place where you can dive into the journey of this meditation. You'll find that it is similar to the meditation you did before in the compass section of this chapter. They are essentially the same, but if that was a swim in the shallows, this is a dive into the deep. Having tried both, you can choose your depth for the other meditations later.

◆ MEDITATION EXERCISE ◆

When you are ready, close your eyes and breathe in light from above into your heart and then, with your exhale, breathe it out in front of you. Only about six feet. Notice what you experience of your space when you imagine it. Close your eyes, go in, and come back when you're ready.

On your next breath, see in your imagination the opening of a gateway in front of you. This is a gateway that connects you to mystery. The unknown. Let it appear however it appears to you. If you need help, use your recollection of the illustration at the beginning of this chapter as a start. Hold it in your imagination. See it hovering in front of you.

Breathe in and ask a question silently in your head: "What is in front of me?"

Breathe out and visualize yourself sending that question into the gateway.

Move your attention into an empty space on the other side and let what answers, answer.

Notice what arises. Anything, everything, is a part of the vision.

Experience it. Notice how it makes you feel.

Take as many cycles of breath to experience the vision as you would like.

When you are ready to move on, breathe in and move your attention into your heart. Ask, "How do I feel?"

Breathe out and relax into it.

Take a few cycles of breath on your own just connecting with the feelings in your heart.

Notice whatever feelings arise. Notice where there is hope and where there is fear.

Notice other emotions, sensations. Any experience is information.

Take your time. Let the feelings come.

When you are ready, breathe in and gather up the feeling in your heart as best you can.

Breathe out and send the feeling up to your head. Ask, "Why? Why do I feel this way?"

Let your mind look for an explanation. What thoughts make sense of the feeling?

Find the words to describe the feeling and send that question into the gateway with another cycle of breath.

Experience a vision again and cycle as many times as you would like.

Notice how the visions, the feelings, the thoughts evolve and produce a story.

When you are complete, open your eyes and take a note of what came through.

If you would like, find a way to express it in outer creative form.

You have turned on the creative engine of a visionary. ◆

This is a powerful current to hold. It is held not with strength but with balance—in motion through cycles. Just as you cannot inhale and exhale at once, you cannot speak and listen at the same time. One at a time. Head. Gateway. Heart. To go deeper, you will need to relax more deeply into the current as it cycles between each point of the triangle. Let the current take you. The more you let go, the more it will flow. The same can be said for how I've presented it to you. Don't hold onto the details of this meditation or the details of each chapter's gateway illustration too tightly. As you build your own relationship with your own creative vision, let it guide you and let it happen how it wants to happen.

The current you are accessing has no limits. It is the engine of inspiration, the light of attention, the generator of genius. This is a form of the same cycle of focus people turn to in prayer. It is akin to the source of prophecy and invention, the very stuff of ideas—more powerful than an atomic bomb, because the atomic bomb itself was born from an idea. Your creative vision is the bridge to the infinite. You stand at the gates. There is no limit to the power of creation's currents, only a limit to the capacity of the channels that hold it. The longer you hold it, the more potent the ideas you come back with will be—but the less sense they will make to others. It is a fine line between brilliance and madness, drawn by the space between a limitless experience and limited words. Like the words of an oracle, the most potent creative visions make little sense when facing the future, but become obvious when part of the past. Hindsight is clearest, but vision is the most penetrating. Which of these governs the world you see?

A Lesson

Seeing Is Believing

A lesson plants a seed.

Creative visions are challenging to share. They are powerful, but highly abstract. They can easily slip through the fingers of the mind and be forgotten without something more tangible to hold onto. That is why we have symbols. Symbols are like gateways between people. If the vision of a gateway connects you to your inner self, symbols do the same to connect you with others. You can gaze at a symbol in front of you and it will open up visions just the same as contemplating a gateway in your imagination. People rally around symbols, sharing in a belief of the visions they bring. This is the power of brands, logos, flags, and icons. Gods and goddesses. Born from highly charged creative vision, they command and focus attention of the masses to form a future built by shared belief into which we all can journey together.

Symbols are the alphabet of nature's language and the voice of the unconscious. Our use of them penetrates deeper than what we humans choose to see. It is the language of creation itself, rendered by color, pattern, and form. That most humans associate the color red with the hopes of passion and the fear of danger is not a construct of shared human imagination alone. It's consistent with what the color communicates among animals and plants in the gardens of the wild. In the ripeness of a fruit, red can be an invitation, but on a shiny leaf, a warning. The red chest of a hummingbird attracts the desire of mates, but also wards off rivals, implying power to both. The redness of a ladybug and tree frog wards off predators who see it and assume poison. The potency of such assumptions evolved the harmless milk snake to mimic the red patterned stripes of the coral snake who actually carries deadly poison.

Beyond color and pattern, the form of the snake itself evokes its own visions of passion and poison beyond the animal kingdom and into the human realm. The symbol of the snake on the tree represents medicine across all modern human cultures, yet it evokes the myth of the serpent who lurked on the tree of knowledge in the garden of Eden, tempting humanity to taste its forbidden fruit. Ripe, red, full of promise but once bitten, the cause of humanity's fall. Consider how a hot red sports car with the logo of a snake conjures the vision of living fast and free as the sexy, dangerous stud on the road of life. Consider how the logo of an apple bitten, inscribed upon the back of a device, invites you to taste all the knowledge of the world for the price of your attention.

Color into pattern. Pattern into form. Form into symbol. Symbol into brand. Visions full of meaning find their way in front of you, guiding you toward the future they invite, if you would believe them. Seeing is believing. Belief is the interest that lifts fortunes. The attention you give these visions is what makes them real. Whether produced by an artist, a priest, an inventor, warlord, or a merchant, symbols guide the direction the masses follow. When a symbol holds what people value, it becomes a brand.

If you want others to value the creative visions you see, start by connecting your vision with symbols. Symbols hold the intangible meaning of a creative vision into a form that binds its story into a memorable brand. Meaning condenses into matter, story into stuff. Leathers, synthetics, rubber, foam, and plastic . . . That stuff gets assembled into a sneaker. Feelings get condensed into story. Michael Jordan wins the 1988 NBA slam dunk competition in a stunning leap from the free throw line, the red jersey of his team flowing in the wind of his flight. A memorable story gets assembled into a symbol. The photograph of the moment of Jordan flying through the air gets rendered into a simplified shape stitched onto a sneaker carrying with it the fierce charge of the color red. That stuff and that story come together to make a brand and a product. Nike's Air Jordan sneakers. Victory used to be a god, but now it's a brand. Nike. The brand is so charged with the energy of perceived value that the first editions of Air Jordan sneakers currently retail at about $17,000. That is enough money to buy a car, or to take a trip around the world, maybe pay off a semester of college or a full year's rent for an apartment. Or put another way, it's enough money to manufacture more than five hundred sneakers with the same stuff.

A powerful brand becomes a powerful magnet of human attention, making any object it's inscribed upon numinous to the point of sacred. Why? Brands become charged with people's hopes or fears. A glowing sign with the symbol of a high-fashion brand inscribed on a city street's wall will have people lining up, eager to step through the door it hangs over. Inscribe a symbol of a conflict-ridden religious or political movement on that wall and the same people will be worked up into the frenzy of a mob to tear it down. Symbols *move* people. They affect action according to the frequency of the energy in their story. People have filled battlefields under the symbol of *their* nation. People have filled stadiums under the symbol of *their* team. The sands of time are also shaped by the stories that travel its tides, whose words are written by the hands of belief. Humans carve the land according to the visions held in the symbols we see.

The power of symbols to move people en masse is a reflection of where the uniqueness of individual experience intersects. You have your own hopes and fears. You have your own story. Your own . . . *thoughts*. Yet, when one symbol is put in front of you and me, it might conjure for us both the same *feelings*. Every symbol put in front of you is like a gateway, one that focuses the light of your attention into a particular story for you to believe. Like a projector of someone else's creative vision in your own, it plays a functional fiction like a movie that evokes the same feelings in everyone's heart, but each of our minds will cast it with different actors according to our unique thoughts. Hearts share a dream. Heads divide it. Many of our most powerful symbols cast their stories from a collective unconscious we share. These most potent symbols act like gods. They may not have the power to move the winds or the seas, but they do have the power to move you and me.

It lies in the power of likeness. The closer a form matches the essential symbol of deeper meaning, the more it carries its vision forward. Thoughts and feelings are the space and time of your inner world. The marriage between them births energy and form. If a symbol focuses your attention to the same frequency of your belief in a god or myth or religion or nation, it will evoke that same energy within you and whatever thoughts and feelings it carries. Consciously and unconsciously. Why else did ancient rulers masquerade as gods and print their face on their empire's coins? To merge their forms with the sacred symbols that already held people's beliefs.

The most valued brands today rest upon the primordial play with the power of god and myth, drawing from them the energy in their symbols whose stories penetrate deep into our collective consciousness. The motivating force of victory rendered as Nike is just one example of many. Hermès handbags, branded after the Greek god representing the energy of travel and trade. The story of the bitten Apple comes from the myth of Genesis and its lessons of knowledge. Even accidentally, the Tesla logo formed to look like a T and a cross section of an electric motor evokes the symbol of Mjolnir, hammer of Thor, Norse god of lightning.

Even the very measure of value that underwrites the economic might of all these brands is upheld by the power of god-wielding symbol. The standard bearer of global currency, the US dollar, is inscribed with the symbol of an illuminating eye hovering atop an Egyptian pyramid underneath the Latin words *annuit cœptis*, meaning, "God has favored." It's called the All-Seeing Eye of Providence, representing the vision of the "one true god" at the foundation of the Western world's self-determining mythology. Evolved from the Eye of Ra, Egyptian god of the sun whose myth tells a story of the life-giving power of the light of attention, the symbol of the dollar is a rebrand carrying a modern vision. The eye of an all-powerful monotheistic god, the "great creator" whose vision oversaw the march of civilization from Egypt through Greece, Rome, and into modernity's promise of a brighter future.

It's like a symbol for the story of creative vision itself, printed on trillions of papers, perpetuating a shared belief: What the Eye of the Dollar sees has value. People follow where it leads, kingdoms and cultures rise and fall, nations change, and the very ground of the earth we walk upon is reshaped by people following where the creative vision of the dollar leads. "Money is everything," some people say. Others say "money is the root of all evil." Money is just a story, but it's the newest version of one that's very old, one that represents the essential functional fiction of creative vision at the heart of building empires. It's as old as belief. Money might be the patron of the arts, but creativity is the mother of money. That's what seeing fortunes means.

The world needs stories. Your vision is the gift that brings them. It goes where you pay attention. Your entire future is laid out in front of you to make with it. The Seven Directions system begins with the direction of *what is in front of you* for good reason. It is the direction that awakens your creative vision, peels back the lids covering your own all-seeing eyes. The skills you've cultivated in this chapter, for this direction, can be applied to all others. You have learned how to connect head and heart to the gateways that lead toward deeper mysteries of the unknown creations *you* can bring to the future. You have learned how symbols, like gateways, are portals to the deeper realms of the unconscious. You have learned how to turn on the engine of creative vision to power your own inner genius. Before you can take the journey to where your true north leads, first you must see it. Now you have many ways to answer what was once a simple question and to follow where it leads. What do you see?

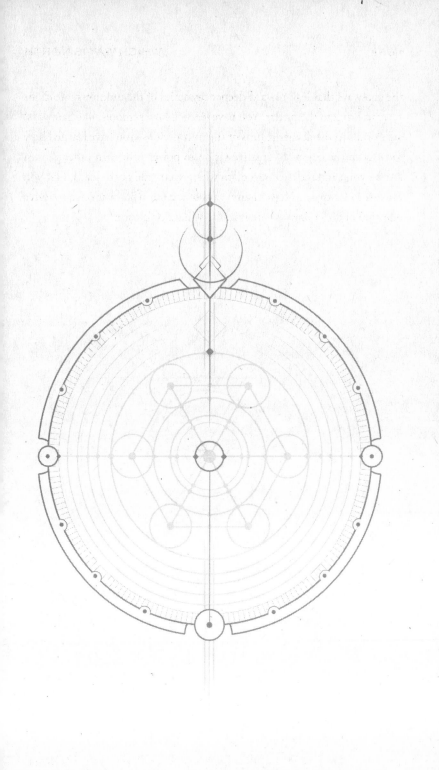

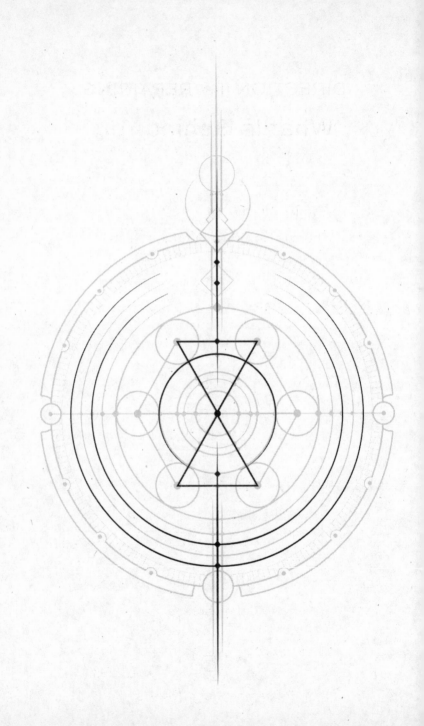

What Is Behind You

There Is No Growth Without Repair

We All Walk with the
Same Monsters

Repairing: Between
Joy and Anger

The Perseid Meteor Shower

Remembrance

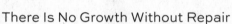

Remember Your Dreams

●

A Point

There Is No Growth
Without Repair

A point starts somewhere.

Something is behind you. Can you feel it?

Don't look because you can't see it; but it is there. Close your eyes and feel that energetic sensation on the back of your neck. Feel that sensation pulse down your spine. Yes, there is the presence of something. While seeing in front of you requires creative vision that pierces through the fog of uncertainty, seeing behind you requires creative vision that pierces through the shadow of forgetting. You grow into your future. You can only repair your past. There is no growth without repair. We all have a reason to grow. We all have something to repair. The lines you draw between these two write the story of what you do here with your time. Every waking moment begins with a story about who you are, told by where you come from and where you are going. As this moment begins, ask yourself: Who are you?

What is behind you is about the power of story, not through imagination, but in remembrance of things past. Your life, as long or as short as it may feel, holds a deep well of energy embedded in moments you can draw from your memories of them. Love them, hate them, just notice how they make you feel. Those feelings are full of energy you can use to create. Emotion is energy in motion. For many, the fog of the future and the shadows of the past seem to be crawling with anxieties. Along the spectrum of hope and fear, joy and anger are powerful feelings often experienced as paralyzing anxiety. What if your anxieties are the source of your gifts? I believe this to be true. I believe anxiety is creativity ready to be transmuted. When I share this idea with people, they often joke back that they have plenty of the anxiety part going on, but not the creativity. They don't believe they can be creative at all. We'll talk a bit more about whatever anxiety is troubling them and soon enough it becomes clear how utterly creative that anxiety is. The frenetic stories anxiety comes up with can be nothing short of ingenious when looked upon with the warm smile of a creative intent. How, *how* did you come up with such a story! Truth can be stranger than fiction, but nothing is more clever than the epics we drum up in our heads. Everyone's anxiety story is unique. Therein lies the key.

Anxiety guards the gate of genius; and also keeps its key. It's just that the guardian feels like such an overwhelming beast sometimes. Well, it would make sense if anxiety is like a three-headed dog because I've found that it loves to play fetch with ideas. When tossing a question in any direction of life—what's in front of me, what's behind—anxiety will come racing back with something. Sometimes, that something is an idea that's actually interesting enough to make with and share. If everyone's anxiety is unique, then those beasty little stories and neuroses that place you at the center of the universe's great concerns bring you something truly special indeed: *original thinking.*

People treasure original thinking. Original thinking is the shine we look for in the brightest creations. It is the sacred people point toward but are too afraid to speak when they use words like *authentic* instead. We look for its emotional charge in the genius of art, culture, and innovation.

We look for it to bring light to the shadows we face. Whatever you choose to do with the unique stories it tells, the generative power of anxiety can be used to bring light to the shadows you face behind you. A domain of experiences past that belong exclusively to you. Anxiety guards the gate, but it guards it for you. It invites you, sometimes drags you, past and into the caves where your deepest memories are hidden. Are there treasures hiding in there among the monsters? I think so. In fact, I think the monsters are just tricks of the shadows who disappear when you turn on the light. What is behind you? Come with me. Let's walk in.

We All Walk with the Same Monsters

A vision inspires action.

I tried to sit quietly on the plywood steps next to his workshop in our basement, but the soft scrape of my nylon soccer shorts against the grain gave me away. It was summer so I was dressed for playing outside, not sneaking into basements. He didn't turn around at the sound, but I knew he heard me. He'd been standing there silently wrapping leather animal hide around the wooden shaft of a spear taller than me, taller than him.

"Do you know what this is?" my father asked me without turning from his work over the leather and wood. I leaned a bit to glance at a different angle over his shoulder and could see he was now tying an eagle feather to it. His workshop light shined a golden glow that cut the dank darkness of this basement that had always terrified me with its strange creaks and cold dusty smells.

"A weapon?" I answered shyly.

"This is a *bear* spear." He emphasized the bear part. He fastened the hide onto the shaft and rocked the spear from side to side, letting it fall from one hand to the other. "It's not a weapon; it's a tool." He motioned over toward the shadows at the far end of the basement. "For walking into the darkness." He pointed the tip of the spear into the dark, past the glow's horizon from the lamplight. My eyes followed toward the edge of the shadow's reaches. I felt a slight chill on the back of my neck as its hairs raised. I was terrified of that place over there.

Like any family, we stocked the shelves of our basement with the kinds of things you don't need to see every day. We kept the normal sort of things you'd expect to find in any basement, like cans of WD-40 and boxes of cereal. We kept abnormal things too. The kind of things you wouldn't expect. The kind that would fill the imagination of a little kid like me just trying to fetch a can of soda with monsters. Things like my grandfather's relics taken from behind enemy lines in World War II. Bayonets, empty artillery shells, and trinkets branded with sinister symbols. He'd stolen them from the palaces of Nazi generals in his service as a Jewish spy undercover in Germany. They were weapons of the physical and the spiritual kind. The acrid smell of a dark history that wanted to hurt people like me. The more I learned about where they came from, the more my stomach twisted.

Halfway into that basement's shadows, we had a pull cord that turned an overhead light on and off. Whenever I *had* to go down there, my little feet would slowly quiver and creep from the glow of that workshop lamp. My thin arms would stretch to reach for the cord to light the rest of the way, protecting me from the shadow's touch. Walking ahead, trying not to look up at the gross collection of dead bugs in the ceiling light's translucent panel, I'd venture the rest of the way past those shelves, grab what I needed, and *sprint* as fast as I could back to the stairs out of there, grabbing and pulling the cord mid-stride along the way. My heart would feel like it was leaping out of my chest to get out of the basement before me.

I would try my best to outrun the feeling of a chasing monster's humid breath making the hairs on my neck stand as it lurched for me.

The scraping sound of my father's shoe against the dirt of the concrete floor snapped me back to attention. He turned and looked at me, nodding his head to the side, beckoning me down from off the steps. "You know what's special about the bear spear?" He paused and watched me shake my head. "It reminds you that you're not alone. It protects, but it also connects."

"Connects?"

"It connects you with people. That's why it's not a weapon; it's a tool. Every family has a bear spear in their past whether they know it or not. Your family comes from England, Germany, Czechoslovakia, France. All around Europe. You've got deep Celtic and Druid roots. Back there and then, a long time ago, back to your—*our*—family's beginnings, the bear spear was important if you wanted to survive in the woods."

"Lots of bears, I bet." I smirked.

"That's right. Lots of bears. Walking around with one of these made sure you were good and protected and that your family was too." He winked. "Here, where you stand, on this ground in America." He beat the base of the spear against the ground a couple of times gently. "They had bear spears."

"Everyone had bear spears?"

"Everyone had bear spears. That's why it connects. We all walk with the same monsters."

We all walk with the same monsters. I turned away from him and looked into the shadows behind me. He took his eyes off the spear and fixed them on me. "Do you know how to use a bear spear?"

"You throw it." I smiled as I mimed a toss.

His belly threw a laugh. "No. Sorry, kid. I don't think you could throw this very far." He tipped the spear toward me to remind me of its height, just over six feet tall from base to tip. "You walk with it." He let that phrase sit, watching me try to understand. "You *walk* with the understanding that what's in the shadows can't really hurt you. Even death can't really hurt you, if you don't let it. Sometimes you need to walk into the shadows. Sometimes you need to look for the monsters that look for you. It's just like walking through the woods to hunt a bear that's also hunting you. When you find the bear, you lay the spear down on the ground."

He crouched down below the level of my eyes to place the spear on the basement floor. "But *hold your grip*," he emphasized as he slightly jolted the shaft of the spear with both his hands. "You plant its base against your foot or against a rock, if you can." He craned his neck around to draw my attention to where he'd wedged the spear's base against the side of his planted foot. I grinned as I saw his face redden with a blood rush from the effort. "Don't let the spear move. Let the bear come to you. You have to be ready to make yourself the bait." He paused and stared at me sternly through his glasses. Those glasses that would steam when he exerted himself. "Face it as it charges at you, and just at the moment the bear stands up to drop on top of you, quickly raise the spear!" He straightened his legs and shot up to abruptly raise the spear. I could see a smile breaking underneath his graying blond mustache. "It falls down and it kills itself with its own weight."

"You have to be the bait," I whispered back.

"You have to be *willing* to be the bait," he emphasized. "To know you are ready to die, if that's what it takes." He nodded. "That's strength. *That* is how you walk with shadows." He tilted the spear forward, handing it over to me. I reached out and wrapped my fingers around the smooth leather of its tightened hides, felt the tickle of the eagle feather on my wrist. Standing in the pool of golden workshop light, I turned toward the shadows and took a deep breath in.

That is a memory from my past I often greet when I walk through the gate and into the shadow of what's behind me. I often even revisit that basement in my dreams. In the darkness of my grief over my father's untimely death, the loss of our family home, our dogs, and the following failure of my mother's health that ultimately took her, too, memories like these were veiled to me by anger. Too much ugliness, too much hurt, too much anxiety to touch these treasured moments that had become wounds.

Then, on a night before my wedding for which I had no parents to attend, I gripped that bear spear and silently watched the moon. The safe glow of the moonlight cut the shadows of a California desert a far walk across the country from the house that bear spear and I were both made in. I faced the memory of its meaning. The sharp fangs in the grimace of my grief stared back. I cried, then I smiled, then I laughed. The grief laughed with me and hugged me like my dad. My anger melted into joy and I thanked him for the wedding gift. We shook hands and I walked forward to make the future of my family, knowing the treasures I carry into it from its past. In the heaves of those lonely cathartic breaths, I felt filled with gratitude for all of it and filled with courage from it. I began to understand who I really am and therefore what I can create.

When my wife and I got wedding tattoos, I included a bear spear on my right wrist. Whenever I shake hands with anybody, I *remember* that I carry, not a weapon that divides, but a tool that connects. We all walk with the same monsters. My creative purpose, my inheritance, is to turn those monsters into gifts. That's the power hidden in the shadows of my past. Let's walk together and see what awaits you in yours.

A Compass

Repairing: Between Joy and Anger

A compass sets direction.

What is behind you is a landscape of untapped energy. In the shadows of your forgetting are aspects of your story worth remembering. The idea of "repair" is about mending. Re-pairing is the act of bringing together connections that were once broken, awakening the power in a machine. A broken connection can be a wound you keep in the shadowy places of your past. A broken connection can be a triumph you left behind in the shadows of your forgetting. A life, for anyone who has had the privilege to live it, is an abundant resource of energy to draw from to make wonders with in this very moment here and now. No matter how you have lived, you have a past. Mistakes. Wounds. Triumphs. All are memories that keep an energy for you to tap, if you are willing and able to find them again. Your past can be a gift, if you would accept it.

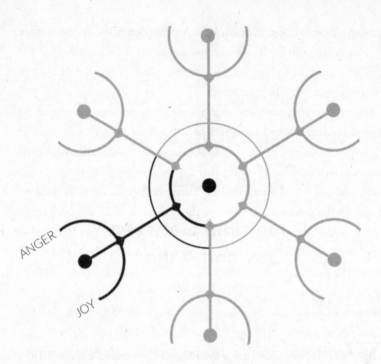

The facts of the past are written, but the stories we tell about them can change. You can walk backward into the dark; you can re-approach your memories from a different angle, like seeing through the reflection of a mirror. Creative vision is the light you bring with you to reawaken the cold memories in the dark with the warm reflection of a story. As you journey backward, there are two energies to navigate between. In front of you, you have your hope and your fear. Behind you, these are flipped in reverse to become joy and anger.

Joy is the attractive energy behind you, felt like the gratitude that arises in an inhale of sweet air. Breathe in to get closer to the feelings of joy behind you. It is those memories of the times when your hopes came true. The kind of moment you just want to breathe in again. To reexperience those moments when you glimpsed your own greatness, were shown your worthiness for love, is to re-pair yourself with those feelings. Your heartbeat quickens. Your face flushes. An emotion rises to the surface of your face. To your body, it's like you are there. It's a miracle that the energy of a moment in the past can be brought forth to the present in replay from your heart to your mind.

Anger is the repulsive energy behind you. It is as discomforting as the feeling of holding empty lungs. Just as it requires courage to sit without air, it requires courage to sit with anger. Love lost. Betrayals. Your own mistakes as well as those of others that cost you. Wounds of the physical, mental, emotional, and spiritual kind. These are the monsters like Medusa that lurk in the shadows and become the objects of your fear because of the anger and the rage they have the power to unleash. You must tread carefully around these inner monsters, it's true. Look upon them directly and it can be paralyzing. Take with you the bear spear. Take with you the sword and the shield. Take with you the promise that you do not walk alone with monsters and that there is triumph for those who do. The world is full of proofs of the power of vulnerability. So many great artists and inventors were propelled by the repairing of wounds from their past. It is in those old wounds that you can claim the magic of the story that is uniquely you. We might share myths, but only you can be you.

Why do it? Why journey behind you when what's past is past? Because to know where you are going, you've got to understand where you come from. Staring at the blank canvas of creativity, what is behind you becomes the flow of color and influence of lines that feeds into what you make for your future. What was gone comes alive again as old memories take on new shapes in re-pairings of new stories. Even the identity project of becoming the person we call you is a profound act of creative expression that, if taken with enough care and purpose, could have the power to heal the world in a small, but worthy way. As humans, we have an existence in time unique to so many other forms of life. Not only can we be abstract into the future, but we can learn lessons from the past. All you have to work with is this present moment, but you can bring energies into it from other places in time to enact change. How remarkable is that?

There is incredible energy in both joy and anger. Too much of one or the other can throw you off track. An overabundance of joy, like hope, might push you off the rails into naivety, missing the key moments of challenge or opportunity in the present. An overabundance of anger might paralyze you with a nihilistic disbelief that anything good or favorable could happen again, at the cost of seeing what's open for you in the present. Finding the right balance between both of these energies can propel you, boost you forward with clear lessons toward a savvy navigation through whatever challenge or opportunity is before you. Your creative purpose is powered by your own innate understanding of capabilities and limitations from lessons learned, both good and bad. You carry with you the inner genius only you could have.

Seeing behind you affords you the opportunity to do incredible inner work, recognizing when there is an energy that can be transformed by moving its orientation between the poles of joy and anger. Often referred to as shadow work, the purpose is to work with your unconscious self to uncover parts of you that your conscious self hasn't been facing. It's an act of seeing the facts of yourself from a different angle. Auditing and claiming how you draw those facts together into a functional story. In working with this, you will find that the gifts of confronting your past come from bringing light to the shadow of delusion, not burying your past deeper in lies. It may feel at times that what is true and what is useful are in conflict when writing your personal myth, but the most useful energy of all comes from clearing the channel of delusion so that light shining in can reflect off the power of the truth.

In this part of the Seven Directions meditation, you are turning the lens of your creative vision backward and opening a gateway behind you to initiate such a dialogue between your conscious self and your unconscious self. Consciously, you ask, "What is behind me?" and visualize the gateway opening behind you. What responds through inner vision, voice, thought, or memory is your unconscious self talking back. As with all phenomena that arise in any of the Seven Directions, this affords you the opportunity to grab the curiosity of what arises and ask, "How did you get here?" Turn it around in your creative vision, move it between your head and your heart to see what story you can work with to repair and therefore strengthen. If what comes through that gateway for you fills you with anger, try finding a new detail or way to say it that counters it with joy. Use your breath to guide you.

I recall once leading a complete Seven Directions meditation session and sharing with the group afterward that when checking in "behind me" I felt the presence of people watching over my shoulder, judging everything I did. I felt close to the anger. I felt that anger physically in a tightness over my right shoulder blade. Gently, with a deep breath in, I nudged that energy toward joy and immediately started to feel it in a different way.

The energy shifted from this idea of people looking "over me" because they were judging to looking "after me" because they cared. The joy came flooding in gently and I felt the tension release beautifully. On the other side, it is rare to find yourself looking back and feeling too much joy.

However, the practice of gently guiding that energy toward the other pole can be a powerful tool for revealing the truth of a wound you may have been hiding from yourself with the illusion of false happiness. I've had moments in my practice where I felt called to examine my past relationships (of many types) and discovered that I had let myself be blind to ways that I was mistreated by or was mistreating others. Moving the energy from feeling "everything was fine" to "maybe not everything was fine" at a gentle pace with a long breath out enabled me to unlock enormous lessons about myself I hadn't been facing. While difficult, the power that sort of repair work gives is invigorating and life affirming. True healing indeed. Remember, the height of your inhale is the height of your gratitude. The depth of your exhale is the depth of your courage. Use your breath to navigate between the energies behind you.

If you, like me, hold grief in your past, this is the direction where you can feel the love you lost again. Such a blend of both energies, joy and anger, to have lost someone you love. The whole of a human life wrapped up in the anger of losing that connection and the joy of wondrous ways to re-find it; to re-pair your heart to theirs. When I drop into meditation and check into what's behind me, if I need the support, I call forth my remembrance of my parents' spirits behind me. I feel them. I really do. I feel the warmth of my mother's hand on my left shoulder and the strength of my father's hand on my right. The same hand that gave me the bear spear. The bear spear I offer now to you. Take the bear spear, or a sword, or a shield. Take whatever tool helps you to walk backward into the shadow behind you, ready to bring out from it the powerful and blazing insight waiting within the story of your inner truth.

Find which way is north, face it behind you, and take a comfortable seat to begin this meditation.

◆ MEDITATION EXERCISE ◆

*When you are ready, close your eyes and breathe in light from above into your heart and then, with your exhale, breathe it out **behind you**. Only about six feet. Notice what you experience of your space when you imagine it. Close your eyes, go in, and come back when you're ready.*

On your next breath, see in your imagination the opening of a gateway behind you. Beyond this gate are the answers to the question "What is behind you?" Once you go in, take your time and breathe through as many cycles as you want to notice the thoughts, feelings, and experiences that arise in response to that question.

There are no coincidences when you ask the question and move through the gate. Take your time and experience them. If it feels like nothing is happening you can always breathe out and ask the question again and breathe in to see what replies. When you are ready, close your eyes and go in. What is behind you? Come back when you are ready. ◆

A Star

The Perseid Meteor Shower

A star lights the way.

Memories are like the stars in the sky, and stories are the lines we trace to connect them. Stories, like constellations, exist only in perspective. All of the facts in the memories I've shared with you are true. I really did sit on those stairs and watch my father make that bear spear. I still have it today. I can see it as I write. My father really did teach me those lessons about what the bear spear means. That basement really was full of old Nazi artifacts that were creepy as hell (even if we did have them because I knew my grandfather had played his part in the fight against their regime).

All of these facts on their own might be interesting, but they don't make a story. They need to be drawn together to come to life. Time fades recollection of things past, like my memory of that basement and the sound of my father's voice. Sometimes, the life a story gives memories can impart a useful meaning to help you fulfill your creative purpose. These constellated memories of the story I've shared help me to convey my creative purpose behind teaching how to confront the shadows of your past.

When a story carries a useful meaning like that, it evolves. It becomes a personal myth. As a maker, as a marketer, as a mystic, as a creator of any kind, knowing your myths is essential to everything.

Myths access a deeper place inside of you. Embedded within your psyche, they are part of the unconscious programming of your life's narrative. Just as there are personal myths, there are collective myths in our shared culture that program our collective unconscious. Personal myths are unique to you and can also sometimes provide value to others. Collective myths are more expansive. Like the totem of the bear spear, the myths we share are the constellations that gather the stars of our unique memories to connect us with the broader human experience we can all point to. These stories in our hearts become a bridge to each other across incredible distances of space and time when we see a story that shines a light to us in the dark. They connect us with a soft and friendly whisper like the suggestion that we all walk with the same monsters.

It is our shared myths that pierce the shadows in the sky, painted across the stars with the glow of the meaning we give them. The constellations tell stories. Some constellations burst to life in cosmic theater like the reliable midsummer blockbuster of the Perseid meteor shower that has played in the night of every August through the ages of humankind. The names we give to those clusters of stars are Perseus, Andromeda, Cassiopeia, and Pegasus. They are animated into the retelling of a great shared myth reenacted by the dazzling streaks of shooting stars and how each character's constellated story enters the stage of the night sky as they rise, ready to perform their part in the cosmic play of life. You could say it's just stuff up there. Stones and stardust burning in the firmament. Everything is just stuff until it holds a story. How important must this story be if it was written in the shadows of every midsummer night for as long as humanity can remember. I wonder how many hands have pointed to it from parent to child, sharing its meaning as each generation turns to fall into the shadows of time. That alone is enough intrigue to the myth that makes it worth telling and retelling again and again and again. To sit with this story is to re-pair the present with the past.

The Perseid myth is about the journey we all must take into the shadows to face the wounds of our past and steal from them their power to bring our future into the light. First to rise in the starry sky is King Cepheus and Queen Cassiopeia looking on as their princess, Andromeda, is held captive over the great void with the jaws of chaos threatening to consume her. Andromeda, and the future she carries, is imperiled because of her parents' mistakes. The sins of our mothers and our fathers are the deepest joys and angers of our past. Then rises the hero Perseus from whose constellation's heart the shooting stars flow. As the story is told, Perseus swoops in wielding the power of a monster he defeated in the darkness of a cave. Carrying that power, Perseus is able to rescue Andromeda and the future she represents.

Perseus stole the power from Medusa. A monster formed in the trauma from a tragedy of errors not unlike the ones that imperiled Andromeda. Medusa is a great beauty whose tremendous heart was broken and cursed to be forever hidden behind a gruesome form. Lurking in the depths of a cave, she is the embodiment of the wounds that hide in the shadows of what you keep behind you. The monsters that grow around traumas can become so terrifying that to look them in the eye would turn you to stone. That is the very power Perseus steals. Save your future by stealing power from the wounds of your past. That is the secret at the heart of the Perseid myth. Important enough to write in the sky and pass from parent to child each midsummer. Every generation has wounds in its past. Every person has wounds in their past. How many have the courage to turn those old wounds into new powers?

The complexity of the Perseid myth and others like it is astounding. Every little detail is a thread that leads to a deeper lesson among a tapestry of so many more. You can pull on any part you like and find where the collective myth becomes personal, where the lessons for everyone become yours. What was the mistake that made Andromeda a victim? What was the tragedy that made Medusa a monster?

A myth holds the subtle technology of a story as told through the interaction of characters, symbols, and gods, each representing lessons learned from the facts of life against nature's forces. Myths are vessels to transmit through time a human treasure equal and complementary to the value of knowledge of the mind. Understanding of the heart. The act of telling the Perseid myth opens a bridge between hearts to connect. An opportunity for a parent to reveal to their child the mistakes and tragedies of the past. An opportunity to repair them. An opportunity to romance ourselves and each other by becoming our own heroes. An opportunity to learn the wisdom from experiences we don't yet have.

Perseus defeated the monster of Medusa with the help of a shield he used as a mirror and the sharpness of a sword given to him by his father. With the mirror shield, he was able to journey backward into the shadows and approach the monster Medusa without looking at it directly. With his faith in the sword that had won his father so many epic battles, Perseus was able to behead the monster cleanly. When you are journeying backward into the shadows of your past, it is perilous to approach your traumas directly. Approach them from a different angle, like the reflection of a mirror, to see them from a new perspective that helps you to get closer to them safely. Then, with the confidence of a sword that reminds you that we all battle monsters, conquer your shadows and bring their power into the light. It was when Perseus struck down Medusa that the Pegasus leaped out of her, a winged horse of unfathomable power. A unicorn, the very symbol of imagination. The monsters of your shadows become the gifts of your genius. Anxiety becomes creativity.

There is so much power in claiming your vulnerability. Myths are more than lessons for learning; they are blueprints for being. It doesn't just come from a personal myth of mine; it comes from a shared myth for us all. We all share a past just as we all share a future, if we would only save it together.

A Journey

Remembrance

A journey brings experience.

How do you share a moment that has passed? Or create an imaginary one entirely?

If you were to hold a moment in your hand, you would feel it is made up of sensory experiences bound together with the story that gives it meaning. Touch, sight, hearing, smell, and taste. Those detailed memories of a moment constellate together into a story you can point toward to share the experience of it. You give what you know to help someone else understand. You may be able to briefly describe that moment as something like "my first kiss" or "the first time I stepped up onstage," but that is not the experience; that is just the fact of it. If you are creating a story from imagination, the dynamic is just the same. It might be a new moment, but it is drawn by old experiences, no matter how fantastical.

When turning your memory into creation, you will need to pull from your senses. Just as there are senses that help you to navigate outer space, there are senses to help you navigate inner space. In the realm of imagination, where you conjure up scenes in your creative vision, there exists in this moment the smell of your family's kitchen on your favorite holiday. The sound of singing on your birthday. The feeling of another's lips on your own. The details stay with you. Those details can be given. They are the riches of phenomena to treasure in a meditation. The tiniest particle of dust floating across your vision reminds you of the smell of your old pet's dander warmed by the Sunday morning light on the carpet. Suddenly the sizzle of bacon crackles out from the kitchen behind you and you turn to smile at the apparition of someone you love who has long since gone. You feel an ache in your heart as something cracks open when you see, hear, smell, and feel a moment that was once yours and yours alone become eternal because in expression it can be given. Having the capacity to turn a memory into art adds a whole new purpose to living. Joy is infinite. It only grows when it is shared, at the cost of no one.

Share your joy. Like everything with creative vision, there is a muscle to recollection you can strengthen if you train it. To deepen your ability to reexperience and re-pair your heart with a moment in the past, let's deepen your ability to call it back into the present. Sit comfortably and, when you are ready, drop into this meditation.

◆ MEDITATION EXERCISE ◆

Breathe in deeply for a count of seven.

Hold your breath for another seven.

Breathe out. Count to seven.

Again, but deeper. In. Hold. Out. One more time.

There is a reason I consistently begin meditations with this breathing exercise.

It helps to clear you of whatever residual feelings you might be holding onto, even if you aren't aware of them.

The rhythm of your heart is regulated by the rhythm of your breathing.

The patterns in both are drawn from the memory bank of rhythms that are like a music book scoring all of the characters you've played in your life.

Every character has a song. Every character has a feeling.

Some feel more tensed up than others. Some feel more relaxed.

That argument from last night, or those joyous moves you busted out on the dance floor, or even that news story you saw, they brought with them a feeling that sticks around in your body.

Each with their own heartbeat. Each with their own way of breathing.

You want to clear that out before getting creative with feeling.

So again, breathe in deeply for a count of seven. Hold your breath for another seven.

Breathe out. Count to seven.

Repeat, but make it your deepest breathing so far today. In. Hold. Out. One more time.

Now, scan through your body and notice everything you feel inside of you.

Where do you feel tension? Where do you feel release? Is there an ache? Is there a tickle?

Start from the top of your head and slowly work your way down through the neck to your shoulders.

Move into your arms and out to your fingers. Back to your shoulders and down through your chest and back and into your belly, your hips. Down through your legs and into your feet, your toes.

Can you feel your heart beating through it?

Close your eyes and be with these feelings, then come back.

Now, scan through the surface of your skin.

How does the air feel on the back of your neck? Your cheeks, forehead, all of your face?

How do your clothes feel where they are touching your skin? Are they coarse or smooth? Warm or cool?

What about your forearms? Your hands? Your legs? Your feet?

Notice the sensations on the surface of you.

Close your eyes and be with these feelings, then come back.

Now, what do you taste in your mouth and in your nose?

What do you smell? Don't concern yourself with what these scents might mean or where they come from.

Just be with their texture, their feeling.

Close your eyes, explore these subtle sensations, and then come back.

Now, listen to the sounds around you and inside of you.

Listen without judgment.

Don't try to figure out what the sounds are or what they mean. Again, just be with their texture.

Can you feel their vibrations on your eardrums? Can you feel their vibrations on your body?

Starting with whether you can hear your breath, or your heart beating, or your tongue swallowing.

What sounds can you hear from in front of you? Behind you? To your left? To your right? Beneath you? Above you? How far away can you hear?

Close your eyes and be with what you hear, then come back.

Last, you will look up and stare blankly and evenly at the sights around you in your field of vision.

Just notice the color, the hue, the patterns and textures of light painted before you like art on a canvas.

No judgment, just experiencing.

Look up, eyes open. Be with what you see, then come back.

Breathe in deeply again and sigh it out whenever you are ready.

This is the moment. Here. Now.

Each of these experiences comes together into a constellation of feeling that connects into the story of right now. ◆

How would you capture and express the moment you just experienced? How would you get the inside of it out? Think up some adjectives that you would use to describe each of the senses and write them down. These are the keys to turning the joys of your life into art.

How would you describe what you felt on the surface of your skin?
How would you describe what you felt inside of your body?
How would you describe what you smelled?
How would you describe what you tasted?
How would you describe what you heard?
How would you describe what you saw?

All of these questions are invitations to respond with something evocative to mint the memory in higher refrain. It might be a challenging exercise at first, but the more you do it, the more you will build a vocabulary of sensory experience—however you express it. Words, symbols, images, sounds, the very stuff of sensory experience itself build out this vocabulary as you render and re-render your experiences with them.

Your life is full of its random-access memories, floating freely behind you unbound to any timeline. A culture is too. We have a shared memory. As your personal myths are nested within the broader collective myths, so, too, are your personal memories a part of the collective. Great art, resonant creativity that speaks to the masses, does so because it speaks for the masses. How often do you come upon some work of music or film that feels like it's written from your own nostalgia? Every life has its moments, every culture has its waves. Your memories are a droplet within them, intermixed with mine and everyone else's as we move together through the river of time. Even the most intimate of experiences in your life reflects something in someone else's. Heart to heart, a shared recognition of what it feels like to have lived. The spark of recognition in having memories is the reminder to remember what holds us together over what sets us apart.

In art, there are two sides to how the creation of your vision can be experienced. Your creative vision can be *expressionistic* if it is rendered in such a way that captures your inner experience in making it, even distorting the objective reality of form to capture it. Your creative vision can also be *impressionistic* if it is rendered in such a way that orients the audience's experience of beholding it, often adhering strictly to the forms of objective reality to capture it. Whether your creativity is about your expression or your audience's impression, the measure of its impact comes from your vocabulary of sensory experience.

In the trade of creative strategy, makers and marketers will very often construct what is called a "mood board" to evoke the feelings of an experience we are creating—be it some kind of storytelling content or immersive experience. These are a collage of sensory experiences that capture an understanding of an idea. Usually we use images that capture the color, tonality, and feelings that altogether capture the mood we are trying to evoke in our audience. For content (like a film or story) there is also a storyboard that articulates the rough sketches of how the story will be experienced. I've even gone so far as to write "mood stories" for events to capture a fictional first-person perspective of what it might be like to come upon and walk through the space we've created.

Essentially, the practice of expanding your sensory vocabulary helps you to connect with yourself and with others. It becomes a basis for empathy in your creative vision. By going into the cave of your inner experience and deepening your relationship with yourself, you come back out into the light with an ability to hold a deeper relationship with others.

A Lesson

Remember Your Dreams

A lesson plants a seed.

How did you get here? Where you are right now? What were you doing before that and how did you get there? And before that? And again, before that?

Continue remembering backward, taking note of every place you've been today, what you were doing in those places, how you moved between them, and what you did along the way. Keep remembering backward through all of the details you can recall until you get back to the place and time you woke up from your sleep to start today. Do you remember how you woke up? Do you remember how you slept and what you dreamed? Do you remember what you did right before going to bed? Think through everything you did and every place you went yesterday. Keep going back through your memory to the day before that. Hold the continuity. Keep going back and back and back as far as you can remember without breaking the thread of your lived experience from one moment to the next. Follow the path of where your feet have taken you, where the vehicles you've ridden have traveled. Remember the chairs you've sat in, the doors you've walked through, the places and things you've seen. Think back to the foods you've eaten and to the drinks you've drunk. Remember the people you've been with, the hands you've shaken, the conversations you've had, in person or not. Keep going back, back, back, pulling on your memory's thread until you can't go any further without forgetting. How far back can you go before your ability to remember conscious continuity breaks? What hides behind that?

Most of us don't get very far wandering backward into the labyrinth of life's memories. Many of us can't even make it back to this morning or to yesterday. Eventually, the thread of recollection just . . . ends. You don't truly know how you got here. Retrace your stream of consciousness far enough through the sequence of moments that brought you here and you'll eventually arrive at the shores of forgetting at the face of a vast unconscious sea. Life is but a dream. Row your boat gently.

Dreaming is the key to an awakened life. Everybody has dreams, just as everybody has a past, but not everybody remembers. The murkiness of dreams makes them especially easy to forget. Their memory hangs over you like a morning fog in those first moments that your eyes open to the day. Even the slightest movement, so much as a reach of your arm, and your dream dissipates away. What was once so present in your mind fades entirely. You forget. You forget so deeply, you forget that you forgot. You pick up your phone, you turn on the TV, and you step into the story of your day as it's told to you by screens. Your to-do list, your assignments, take over. How do you know if the story you're living comes from what you're told or from what you dream?

If you want to write your own story, remember your dreams. Dreams hold the architecture of intuition, a domain of creation at its purest and most profoundly transformative. In dreams, you have the power of a god. Whether you know it or not, you write the story. You create everything. The ground you stand on, the characters that pass through it, and the plot that unfolds; all of it is made by you, for you, and through you. In your dreams, you create upon the canvas of reality itself.

There is an ocean of life in the shadows behind you beyond the shores of forgetting. In dreams, the separation between worlds thins when you swim in that sea. You float closer to the realms of myth where the inspiring voices of the muses sing. They offer their visions to all who would carry them to the world of the waking. Why shouldn't you be one to bring such treasures to shore?

Many of humanity's greatest artists have shared that their best creations came to them in dreams. Many of the greatest innovators and thinkers too. What makes them different is they remember to remember what others forget they forgot. They remember their dreams. When they wake up with something beautifully curious, they capture it. They write it down, or they draw it, or they record it. Whatever the language of their creation, they capture the dream quickly, gently, and firmly like a butterfly held in the hand.

You can do this too. There are two levels to a dream practice. They take a moment to learn, and a lifetime to master. Dream journaling and dream journeying. They each contain a set of tricks to bring your consciousness into the realm of your unconscious where you can access the innermost depths of your psyche to engage with the pure creativity that dwells within. In doing so, they will transform what it means for you to be asleep and what it means to be awake.

DREAM JOURNALING

Dream journaling is the first and most basic step toward learning to access the creative power of your dreams. It begins with what you do when you wake up in the morning. If you want to recall your dreams, the first thing to do is nothing. It's remarkable how even the slightest shift in position can cause the memory of a dream to slip away. Just take a moment to relax and hold onto the memory of what you experienced in your sleep. Anchor in on a specific detail from the dream. It could be a symbol or a person, or some kind of sensory experience. You don't need to remember everything about it; just hold onto it as a place to begin the next step.

Keep a notebook and a pen next to your bed, not anything digital that can distract you with other information. When you're awake and have a detail from your dream in your grasp, slowly sit up to grab the pen and paper. Then start to write or draw. Describe the one detail first. You'll find that the rest of your dream will begin to unleash like a flood through the small crack of that one detail. The more times you do this, the more naturally capturing the stories of your dreams will become.

The challenge with dream journaling is that dreams are a nonlinear experience. Writing, however, tends to be a linear narrative, while drawing tends to be a snapshot of a moment. Just do your best to keep up with it as it flows. It doesn't matter if you capture it perfectly. What matters most is that you build your ability to remember.

The regular routine of journaling your dreams is like building a bridge your unconscious knows it can rely on. Once that bridge is in place, it will keep sending you more and more through the details of your dreams. You have genius in there. Let it know you're paying attention. Try journaling every morning for at least a week and then see if you notice a change in how you dream. At the end of a month, look back through your entries and see what patterns unfold. You might be surprised at what starts to make sense when you connect the dots from your dreams. There are patterns in your past that only reveal themselves in the *active* act of remembering. Dream journaling trains you to see these patterns and create from them.

DREAM JOURNEYING

Dream journeying is the next and more complicated step for unlocking the creative power of your dreams. For many, this is incredibly hard. It is the act of realizing that you are dreaming while it is happening so you can take control of it. Similar to dream journaling, there are huge benefits that come from simply trying. In learning to play a more active role in your dreams, you learn to play a more active role in your life.

Dream journeying, also known as lucid dreaming, requires that you pay attention to the details in your dreams to ground yourself into the reality you've created. To bring more consciousness into the life you live while asleep, you have to bring more consciousness to the life you live while you are awake. You have to train yourself to take nothing for granted, eyes open or closed. You question everything to notice anything, specifically whether if, at any given moment, you are dreaming. Are you dreaming right now? How would you know?

There is a practice referred to as a "reality check" that lucid dreamers use to prepare for dream journeying. While awake or sleeping, you train yourself to stop briefly and assess whether you are dreaming. It helps you to habituate the reflex to recognize mid-dream that you are, in fact, dreaming. As an example, when I was first forming my practice, I would write the word *AWAKE* in all caps in marker on my left pointer finger every day. Each time I happened to look at that word, I would do my reality check, which was to try to press the tip of that finger into the palm of my other hand. I knew I was awake if my finger didn't go through my palm.

In dreams your intentions are a higher power than the laws of physics. Over time, I also began to recognize when the word *awake* wasn't there as a clue that I was dreaming. There is something about locating and seeing the details of your hands when you are dreaming. It anchors you in the reality of the dream. It's easy to get excited and wake up only to lose it as soon as you have it. Anchoring in simple details like your hands helps. It's fittingly similar to how virtual reality experiences become more immersive when they are able to render your hands and track your movements with them. Hands are how we anchor our feelings and grab hold of our reality.

Using reality checks to anchor can take months before having your first breakthrough lucid dream and years to make it happen regularly. It is the journey toward learning that matters the most. Striving to lucid dream teaches you to take nothing for granted about your surroundings. You gain the stronger constitution of not needing the comfort of knowing how you arrived at any given moment and all the pleasure of noticing each moment's curiosities that might otherwise pass you by. With practice, you'll find yourself greeting such existential uncertainty with a smile, because you know that once you anchor into any moment, awake or asleep, you are the author of the dream.

There is no creative act greater than becoming the author of your life. It begins with becoming the author of your dreams and it continues with recognizing that the past you carry is, against the reality of this present moment, nothing more than a dream. There is no end, only new beginnings. Every moment is a new beginning with a story you've dreamed up for its past. The difference between a nightmare and a dream is control of the story. That's the great laugh of learning how to remember your dreams. You also remember how to be awake.

As the creator and character at the center of your life, what would you do with more control over its story? Dropped into an empty space as blank as an untouched canvas, it can be challenging to know where to begin. As a maker, as a marketer, as a mystic—as a human, a living being with the potential and therefore purpose to create—what will be that first brushstroke on the canvas of your life? It's okay not to know. When you don't know what to put in front of you, look behind you, where a past full of colors and characters, symbols and scenes, awaits your vision's call.

Creation is remembrance. "What is behind you" is the tailwind of your story. Your creative vision sets the direction and character of the breeze. Where you come from sets the course for where you're going. Together, they draw the lines that write the name of who you are in this moment. Your story is in your hands, whether they hold a pen, a brush, a sword, or a spear. You can make it. You already have.

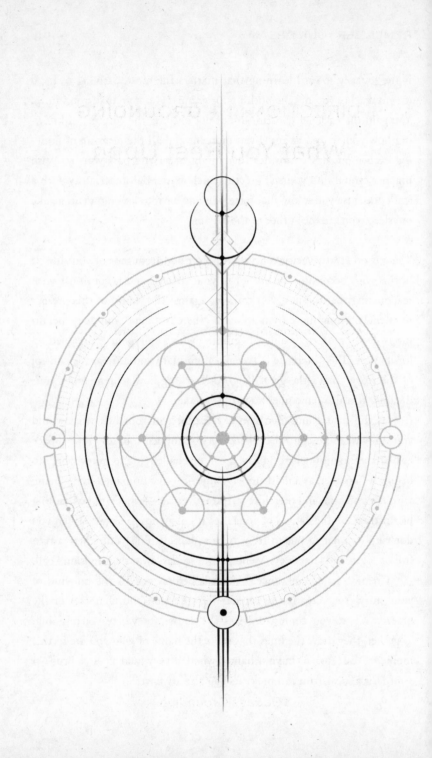

●

A Point

What You're Made of Matters

A point starts somewhere.

Here you are.
Can you feel the weight of your presence dropping into the ground?

You are here. You are made of something. You matter. You rest upon something. It matters. Energy condenses into matter. Your experience of it makes it a story.

"What you rest upon" is the direction of what makes you. It is the ground that holds you. It is the soil of your life, the soil of your land, the soil of your body. It is the soil of your community, your people, your culture. What you make grows from what you're made of.

Creativity needs ground to stand on. Inspiration can come from anywhere and reach anyone, anytime. It can strike like a lightning bolt, but for it to have an impact, it must be brought to solid ground. When a big idea hits, what you're made of and where you stand are the determinants of what you can do with it. How you are embodied in this world affects not only how creativity moves through you, but also how it is received by others from you. How you speak, how you move, how you express your truth are all functions of the soil of life that made you. As is how you are seen and heard. You can say or do or believe anything, but there is the matter of how you are embodied in this world that shapes the expectations that frame you. You can align with these expectations, you can subvert them, you can stretch them, and you can break them, but to do any of that, you must first understand them. What you're made of matters. It is the point from which your creativity flows.

The creative journey can take you anywhere, but your first steps begin with who, where, and what you are. Some of that may feel like a blessing. Some of that may feel like a burden. For all the ground's gravity to weigh you down, its soil also lifts you up. Ground gives you a purpose. The earth wants life to escape it in blooms. That's why it holds you down. To make you grow up. The ground challenges you to defy its gravity.

You might forget the ground you rest upon, but the ground does not forget you. The earth remembers everything. It holds its memories as treasures for those that would dig deep enough to find them. Buried secrets are only secrets to those who don't search for them. Secrets are treasures to those who search, and nothing to those who forget. Dig into the soil. There is magic in the soil always at work, turning waste into life. Nothing created is ever truly wasted on this earth. What lives, lives because of what has died. You live now upon the ground's layers; above rocks and stones and crumbled castles built in sand. You live upon the marks made by hands and feet of those who shaped the earth before you. This is your time to dance and make your marks before the ground covers you too; before your creations become someone else's lost secrets turned into found treasures. The earth remembers everything. It made and will remember you. It's up to you to decide what you will do with the time you have upon it. Will you rest? Will you dance? Or will you fly?

A Vision

Digging into the
Day of the Dead

A vision inspires action.

I liked to run along the old moss-covered stone walls hidden in the backwoods of my New England home that had marked the battlefield lines of the American Revolution. That was the soil of my life.

As a little kid, I'd dig my hands into the dirt and pull back stones to look for trinkets from the stories of the land that made me. Old skeleton keys, thimbles, polished gemstones, even musket balls. Curiosities. They made the myths of patriots and revolutionaries real to me. I kept the best trinkets as treasures, hiding them in one of my dad's old cigar boxes tucked away in the top shelf of my bedroom dresser. They were reminders that I was a small part of a bigger story. Bigger than anyone could imagine. Older, too, as the smoky, sour smell of aged tobacco insisted every time I opened the cigar box to rifle through its secrets. I believed the secrets of those treasures held powers I could only know by asking them. Through them, I explored the far reaches of my imagination.

One day, I stuck my old skeleton key into the ground and turned it, feeling the crackle of cold stones and soil as I did. I had gotten the idea that just from holding the key and asking it to tell me its secrets, it could control the weather. I have no rational explanation for why I thought that, but within minutes of turning the key, the sky started snowing. I looked up and laughed as the snowflakes melted on my nose.

Afterward, I felt afraid to try that again, for fear of testing it. I wasn't sure what scared me more—the idea that the magic was real or the idea that it was not. Regardless, that old skeleton key unlocked in me an important lesson. The magic only happens if you try. The difference between a secret and a treasure is whether you search for it.

Of all the secret treasures I found in the ground I grew up with, the most enchanting were the arrowheads. To come across one of these mysterious etched stone tips was exceedingly rare. I didn't know much about them. I knew they came from a deeper past, buried underneath the topsoil of the stories I'd been told, whispering of stories I hadn't. A deeper myth beyond the shadow of my unknown, underneath the legends of patriots and revolutionaries whose portraits papered my classroom walls. Finding those arrowheads was like finding a tear in the fabric of the American story that I rested upon, revealing other hidden threads underneath. It showed me that there was more buried in the ground on top of which I was living. More than water in the soil that made me.

Your life rests upon a story. That story rests upon something else. You can always dig deeper. There are hidden roots in the soil of the land still speaking, but only coming through in the hush of buried artifacts and forgotten names. You won't be taught every story about the soil that made you. Some would have them stay secrets. Some would have you go find them.

In the years that followed, my curiosity led me to cover a lot of ground searching for a lot of secrets. I became a collector of treasures that tell stories in the form of necklaces and clothes that proudly displayed my knowledge of cultures I had learned about. Some I had read about in books or on the internet. Some I had seen through the window of a car on sightseeing vacations. My enchantment with the treasures of the world became something of an identity as told through the constant collage of my adornments and the magic that unfolds by wearing them.

On a hot summer's day well into my adult career, I found myself in the bustle of yet another conference in what had become a long marathon of weekly networking events. This one, in the middle of downtown Los Angeles, was a summit of venture capital investors, media personalities, social impact organizers, sustainability entrepreneurs, and marketers. What was unique about this conference was its deliberate focus on intersectionality. The representation was diverse, cutting across many borders of culture and definitions of wealth, so the opportunity for meaningful interaction was high—and the community expectations set around it encouraged more thoughtful conversation than transactional networking. When everyone is different, everyone gets to be interesting just by being themselves. That's the vibrancy of potent soil.

This event wasn't designed to be a conference for meetings; it was designed to be a conference for exchanging ideas. It was genuine in the effort. We all tried, with great strain against our networking instincts, *not* to ask each other, "What do you do?" Instead, I found it more fun to ask, "What are you making?" It yields conversations about what makes us feel alive.

I was absent-mindedly watching the painting of a mural and waiting in line for some food when I noticed a tall figure walking toward me with purpose. He was a hulking presence of a man, commanding my full attention when he stopped and stood next to me, towering over me like a bear. His stature was more absolute than it was imposing as his square jaw and flat-brimmed hat framed a gentle smile looking down upon me. He looked to have on him about as many years as me. "I wanted to come over and ask you about your backpack," he shared plainly as he reached out his hand to shake mine. "Where did you get it from?"

"Oh? This? I picked this up across town just the other day." It was a recent purchase I'd made. I'd worn out my old backpacks and laptop cases and wanted something stylish to bring to these conferences. This one came from a leather shop. It had cut up and stitched together these brightly colored patterns from an old wool blanket that reminded me of the family trips I used to take to the Southwest Americas. The pattern reminded me of an old blanket I had purchased at a shop just outside the Navajo and Hopi Reservation as a young kid and still kept on my bed decades later. The backpack felt like the right totem to carry my story as it carried the tools of my travels.

The man nodded his head slowly. "If you're going to wear those symbols, you should understand what they mean," he said. I felt my stomach twist. "I am of the Lakota Sioux tribe. I came here from Standing Rock where we had the protests to stop the pipeline. That symbol on your backpack, it's a symbol from my people. It's called the Morning Star. It is meant to bring courage. It looks like it's cut off about halfway through on your backpack, though, which is strange. We don't normally do that. If you count the corners in the design, though, that tells you the strength of the courage it brings." He paused. "It's also strange that these other symbols are here on it too. These are symbols from different tribes. You don't usually see them together."

"I, well. Thank you," I replied as he calmly smiled. I stirred with an odd mixture of feeling grateful and ashamed. I hadn't even known my ignorance. To me, this was just a pattern. I hadn't even understood there were such meaningful symbols hidden in its design.

"We see this happening a lot. These symbols of ours become fashionable and they appear in places that don't make sense with what they are. There are many symbols and stories that we like to share, but there are others we prefer to keep secret until the time is right. Most of all, we just want to make sure what is out there, people know and understand."

We stood together and shared some silence. Then, for a few moments after, we pointed at and talked about the various symbols we could see around us and what each meant to him and to me. We shared a bit more about each other's stories and parted ways.

Toward the end of the conversation, I returned to the backpack. "What . . . do you think I should do with this?" I asked, having taken it off my back, now holding it in my hands.

"You should just know to understand the symbols and their meanings." That was it. He shook my hand again then turned and walked away.

My only steps from there had to be out of misunderstanding and toward understanding. My knowledge of things was an illusion. I'd only learned through the pages of books and from the other side of a window. It was a call to put my feet on the ground and sink my hands into the soil to understand what the land I walk upon really means. There is a difference between explanation and experience as there is a difference between knowing and understanding. The difference is in the journey.

I headed southwest, back to the Hopi Reservation where I had gotten the blanket bearing its symbol as a child, when my search for treasures in the soil had just began. This time, I didn't gawk at the land through a car window. I had an invitation from a guide who introduced me to his home and his people. I learned from him that symbols are seeds for culture. You can see the spirit of a culture by how it keeps its seeds. Kneeling over a sprouting seedling of corn, he told me about how they grow when you sing to them, showing them you understand their journey and that you care. They rise up to reach toward the warmth of your affection. He shared that this very much embodies how the Hopi see their relationship to the earth and to the rest of humanity. Their culture is about keeping "Creation," a noun that encompasses all of nature, turning for the rest of humanity through the humble act of knowing, understanding, and loving their land.

He brought me to his friend, a jeweler, and walked me through the symbols and their myths. At least, those of which they felt it was okay to share. He brought me to his home and pointed to the ceremonial "kivas," sacred spaces dug into the ground prepared for the year's cycle of rituals and initiations for each rising generation to understand the stories. Three kivas marked the position of the three stars of Orion's Belt. A fourth in

the distance marked the position of the Morning Star, Sirius. The movements of the Morning Star retell the story of creation as it moves through
the seasons every year. It is the guide of ritual and meaning, singing down
upon the people as they sing down upon their seeds. The Hopi, I learned,
see all the other cultures of the world as their children. So long as they
keep their cycle of rituals going on their land, the rest of us will be okay,
whether or not we know why. Quietly holding it down.

I followed the path the Morning Star set beneath my feet through
the hidden Mayan temples of Guatemala where I saw the enormous scale
of the lost cities buried underground. A local guide who had grown up
among them and had studied at the university showed me how the temple peaks align with the stars to mark the seasons. Stand atop one of the
unearthed temples of the lost Mayan cities and you will see across the
jungle a vast landscape of mountains out to the horizon. Those aren't
mountains; those are buildings keeping buried secrets of a deeper story
in the ground. The books would tell you the culture that made America's
temples is lost. The soil that surrounds them would laugh at the idea that
anything needs to be found.

I followed the path the Morning Star took me on, to a city where the
colors of supposed lost cultures still dance on the soil the books say buried them. Oaxaca, Mexico, during its celebration of Dia de los Muertos,
Day of the Dead, is a parade of laughs at the great cosmic joke of being
alive. You can taste the flavors of its certainty. That good soil in Oaxaca
(wu-ha-ka) has given to the world the deeply rich flavors of mole sauce,
the uplifting fire water of mezcal tequila, and the magic mushroom that
has revolutionized consciousness and cultures globally. It is also the home
of the Zapotec, the first people of that land who still today are renowned
for their notable craftsmanship, including beautifully hand-loomed wool
rugs imbued with patterns and symbols designed to carry stories.

Among their most well known, the Morning Star. The symbol of
Oaxacan light. Reminder that the dead are not done. The same Morning
Star symbol that had belonged to other tribal nations to the north, east,

and west, across the American continent the First Nations people refer to as Turtle Island. I was experiencing a deeper story in the soil of the land I call home that defied how it, to me, as a child, had been explained. The supposedly lost culture of the American continent isn't dead at all. It's very much alive and dancing, despite what a stuffy New England school textbook might prefer to say is history. What an odd deception, to push a people out of the present by insisting they belong to the past. Perhaps I was starting to understand something.

The messy mayhem of those Oaxacan parades that wind through its bustling city streets and hallowed groves of graveyards are a reminder that what's living and what's dead are two sides of the same soil of our creation. It's in the dance that old symbols come alive with renewed understanding. What's dead doesn't have to be held in the past and called history, safely pinned to the wall of an air-conditioned museum with a plaque to explain it. It can be experienced instead. It can sweat and dance in the dirt of the present and be called culture. Life is movement after all. Death is the illusion that things are done. There are no endings, only new beginnings born from memories in the symbols we keep as our seeds. People's faces painted with skulls light up candles, string up purple and gold marigold flowers, and leave food and drink next to photographs to invite the spirits of the dead to dance with them. In a parade like that, who can tell the difference between what is and what was when what's dead and what's alive look the same?

In the blurry-eyed dizziness of jumping into a culture's dance, your head gets overwhelmed by the feast of symbols. You're better off taking in the experience with your heart. With the heart's language of color, pattern, and form, you begin to see both sides of the soil that feeds a culture, just as a plant has both its flowers and its roots. A symbol is a flower nourished by roots that give it meaning. In a festival like Dia de los Muertos, a vibrant garden bursts out of the culture's soil and loudly bears the colors of its symbols that have long survived as tenacious seeds to escape the darkness around them and reach the light in full bloom.

The Day of the Dead and its lavish parades arose generations ago as a way to persuade the indigenous people of the land to celebrate the Catholic holiday All Saints' Day, which follows Halloween or (All Hallows' Eve). A holiday of an arriving culture being paved atop the soil. As it is a holiday to remember the saints of the church who are gone and buried in the ground, it is only reasonable for the people to do the same for their beloved family members who have gone too. So it became a time for remembrance and the passage of stories of those gone between generations' hearts. Within the homes of all who celebrate are assembled altars adorned with flowers and offerings of all types surrounding images of their family's dead. Therein lies the tenacity of the seeds. Trace back your family's stories far enough and you reach the shores of legend and myth where the roots of your ancestral culture grow quietly in the deep. To know the old stories, you must understand their meaning. As happens all around the world on All Hallows' Eve, the dead and their symbols come alive in costumes and decoration. The vines of stories of the old weave within stories of the new, and one symbol, one holiday, one celebration can mean at once many different things.

Among the festival of dancing symbols, each a flowering of their own story born from intertwining roots rising out of America's complex soil, I felt myself an outsider. I remembered the lesson of the backpack. If you're going to wear that symbol, you should understand what it means. The Morning Star had sent me on a journey, but I still felt like I was watching from the other side of a car window, a tourist standing on the fringe taking photos to keep in a book. That is, until a very drunk teenager threw his arm firmly around me and shoved a bottle of mezcal toward my mouth, pulling us stumbling together down the street parade. The burning taste of mezcal's nectar of European alchemy entangled with American plant medicine roots seared my tongue. "Viva Oaxaca!" he shouted with the cracked voice of a young man come alive against a late night. Long live Oaxaca. Long live the people.

Taking another sip, I looked down the street in the break between the city canyon walls, and suddenly saw a shimmering star beginning to rise between the murals. It was Sirius, the Morning Star, singing down its light under which, at least for me, old symbols bloomed anew. A glimpsing moment, an experience, to help me understand.

A few weeks later, my mother passed away. I returned home to New England to bury her next to my father. At her funeral, I remembered a line they used to always say to me. Keep on dancing and you'll never die. So, in celebration of my parents, the funeral party went to a concert for my mother's favorite band, the Grateful Dead, carriers of the great American folk music tradition. They were performing at the football stadium for our hometown team, the New England Patriots. Also my mother's favorite. We would watch them play together almost every Sunday. Walking into their concert, I saw the skulls and flowers of the Grateful Dead's iconography that accompany their colorful crowds of fans adorned in tie-dyed shirts, the same sort my mother used to wear every day. It reminded me of the Day of the Dead, but this time it was the dead of mine. It felt like walking among the full bloom of flowers in the garden that made me. The soil of my life. Only now, I understood that these symbols had all come from and been entangled with something much deeper. The continent's tenacious seeds had broken through the pavement of a modern culture laid atop the deeper layers of ground my life, my community, my culture had been built on. We all had been wearing them and calling it "counterculture" in defiance of the mainstream. Perhaps that defiance was born from deeper memories than we knew, buried in the soil we danced upon to the music.

Looking at the symbols all around the concert, I saw the red, white, and blue logo of the American football team and had to laugh out loud as a memory from my journey came back to me. It was the symbol of a patriot made into a heavily marketed brand, channeling my hometown's revolutionary roots into professional sports. The quintessential mainstream. I remembered a moment with the Hopi guide who was taking me around his home village on the reservation. We had stopped at a security check-point at the entrance when I saw the guard was wearing a hat with a symbol on it. "Ah! That's the New England Patriots!" I eagerly exclaimed when I saw it, happy for the first recognition of a symbol from my home in this place. He only shrugged with a puzzled look on his face. My guide turned to me and said, "He doesn't understand what that means."

A Compass

Grounding: Between Pride and Shame

A compass sets direction.

Facing the direction of "what you rest upon" is facing the reality of what you are made of—and what you are not. It is about acknowledging where you are rooted and how that ground, like the soil of the land beneath your feet, nourishes you. This is the ground of your heritage, your community, your platforms. Some of these elements are fixed, and some of them can change.

The land beneath your feet is in constant change. To meditate or contemplate upon the layers of the soil that you rest upon, with all the secrets they keep, is among the deepest ways to cultivate a depth of presence in any place, any moment. It is a call to understand where you are and what your presence means atop its story. Every inch of earth offers something to learn. Nourish it as it nourishes you with the water of understanding.

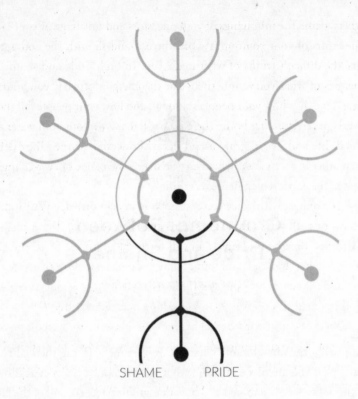

SHAME   PRIDE

Dig down into the soil of "what you rest upon" and you will encounter the attractive energy of pride. Pride sings in the stories and elements that you would proclaim as your heritage, as your lot, as your station. Your belonging in your community and your community's gifts to the world from the culture that shapes it. This is a recognition of your people and their strengths, whatever that means to you. It is a recognition of the soil of your human body, the inheritance that your life rests upon, wherever you take it.

What are you most proud of? What would you draw from your pride that would encourage you to share in story? Breathe in and feel the gratitude for all that makes you what you are. You will also encounter the repulsive energy of your shame. The costs of your privilege paid for by others' pain. The misgivings of your ancestors and misusage of your land. The errors of your community. Breathe out and sit with the courage to face the difficult truths of what made you. In both pride and shame are energies of what you've inherited, not the energies of what you yourself have done. It is how your people stand tall and how your people fall short. Everyone, *everyone* has both. There is no soil made without both water and blood, life and death, growth and decay. Pride and shame. They define each other in an endless alchemic cycle that is the magic of ever-changing being. The earth remembers everything.

To connect with what you rest upon is to acknowledge your indebtedness to both sides. These are the roots that made you. These are your platforms. Breathe in deeply and call forth the gratitude of all the gifts in your bones, muscles, and foundation . . . and story. Breathe out deeply and find the courage to confront the costs of all of those wonderful things. Nothing made is ever wasted, and nothing made is ever free.

There is nothing in the soil of your life that is to your credit or your fault, but it is your responsibility. It is your lot. You get to be here now. You have done nothing wrong by being here in this moment, but you have everything to make right by how you live it. This is *your time* to dance your feet on the ground and shape it. To honor the responsibility and debt of your being is an easy path to your purpose. Something we know is so precious and so hard to find yet is hiding underneath all of our feet. You can find a purpose that draws from the energies of the pride and shame in the water and blood that made you. Your body, your home, your knowledge, your message. Everything in your expression came from somewhere, planted in the seeds of the symbols worn and watered by the understanding of your stories. If you're going to wear that symbol, you should understand what it means. This is the charge of what you rest upon.

When you visit a place, what marks do you leave to shape it? How deeply do you understand the story in the layers underneath the topsoil of that land? Give it the gift of your understanding. Water it with your attention. Get dizzy with the experience of how it dances, with you and without you. You can unlock the secrets of the ground's treasures while also leaving them be. You don't have to take, to play. The pride and shame that reside between us can sometimes feel like a call to inaction. It's easy to seize up and keep the walls between us thick. Understanding knocks those walls down and makes them bridges. Ultimately, we share the same soil together. At the deepest layers, we are entangled in the same roots. Life thrives not from separation, but from interconnection. Expand the circle of your story by embracing the truth of what you rest upon, wherever, whoever, however that may be. Dance on the soil. Give it the breath of life; sing your affection to its seeds.

Wherever you are, whatever you are made from, go deep into the meditation of this direction and see what you can dig up. Turn secrets into treasures. Think of your parents and their parents. Think of their stories. Think of the deeper stories buried in the flesh of your body. When your eyes close, let your creative vision creep down through whatever flooring you rest upon and into the ground that holds it. Think of the layers to the story of that land. Think of your community, be that your family, your friends, your neighborhood, your team, or your business. All of these are, in one way or another, here to hold you as the soil of your life. You are held. What energy can your roots draw from in the charge of what the ground gives you? Find a comfortable place to sit, and let the sense of gravity sink you in. You are here. How deeply can you experience it?

◆ MEDITATION EXERCISE ◆

*When you are ready, close your eyes and breathe in light from above into your heart and then with your exhale, breathe it out **beneath you**. Only about six feet. Let your imagination travel down through the flooring, the infrastructure, the soil, rock, and stone. Notice what you experience of your ground when you imagine it. Imagine how your body rests upon it, made of the same dust and clay. Close your eyes, go in, and come back when you're ready.*

On your next breath, see in your imagination the opening of a gateway beneath you. Beyond this gate are the answers to the question "What do you rest upon?" Once you go in, take your time and breathe through as many cycles as you want to notice the thoughts, feelings, and experiences that arise in response to that question.

There are no coincidences when you ask the question and move through the gate. Take your time and experience them. If it feels like nothing is happening, you can always breathe out and ask the question again and breathe in to see what replies. When you are ready, close your eyes and go in. What do you rest upon? Come back when you are ready. ♦

A Star

The Marketplace of Stories

A star lights the way.

Symbols are seeds. Stories are the roots that branch out from them when watered by understanding. Surrounding a story's roots is the soil of the culture that keeps it. It's the story about the story. No two cultures tend to their soil or their stories the same way. They are as varied as any ecosystem. The soil of some cultures is like a wildlife preserve, best left untrampled and with nothing taken. Some might appear to be barren fields, but under their surface they keep a colorful bloom waiting patiently for their season. A culture, like a land, can be recovering from the wounds of wildfire, or the silence of winter. A culture can be damaged from being overly mined. A culture can be an abundant garden, wanting nothing more than to spread its seeds.

The stories a culture keeps are the basis of its life. They carry within them the codes that hold memories of a past for a future that will someday need them. Stories flourish in the soils that made them, and they become something else when transplanted. The waters of different understandings call forth different memories from a symbol's seeds. Just as the texture of different soils shapes different paths roots will take, so, too, do different stories about a story.

The indigenous American stories I encountered on my journeys are beautiful, brimming with power that unfolds in their every telling, transforming you from the inside out like good medicine. I want to tell them in these pages, but they are not for me to tell for my gain. To do so would be to add bitterness to what is otherwise sweet. The story about those stories in the soil of their culture is that they are sacred and have too often been taken, reshaped, and paradoxically underappreciated for their power while creating great value for those who take them; much like the minerals and plants of the lands that made them. In the Jewish community I grew up in, the culture stories are fiercely guarded. So much so that the foundational community text, the Torah, is kept behind a lavish curtain, and if so much as a single letter's brushstroke is misplaced in the writing of its scrolls, it must be destroyed and the reproduction of it restarted. The story about the stories is one of meticulous preservation against the tides of history.

The global culture of the modern world is a marketplace of stories. Every day millions of pictures, videos, essays, and illustrations are exchanged for attention, for money, or for a chance at a career. The soil of our global culture has suddenly become vastly interconnected, much to the shock of some ecosystems and to the replenishment of others. The waters of understanding mix with the toxic waste of misunderstanding, and misinformation spreads like weeds through the gardens that color our views. The wonder of the earth is that it seems to always keep, even if buried and hidden, a solution to the very problems its own growth creates. The earth remembers everything for a reason. So its stories can someday be told.

Years ago, fresh out of college, I was fortunate to be invited on a trip to Morocco at a time when I was trying to figure out what to "do" with my life. I was in my mid-twenties and made conversation with a man not too far from my own age who was tending to a spice stand with barrels overflowing with exotic old-world flavors. We were in the center of Marrakesh's overwhelming Jemaa el-Fnna market, which, as the beating heart of this storied ancient city, could be understood as the Times Square of a distant age, bustling with travelers like me who'd crossed the desert from their own distant homes to come together in a shared space and time of vibrant exchange.

Holding a pungent bag of dried turmeric, I asked him how long he'd been working at this stand. All his life, was the answer. So I asked him how he'd started. It was his father's, was the answer. So I asked him how his father got started. It was *his* father's, was the answer. Before him? *His* father's. Before him? Again, *his* father's. He smiled. So I paused for a moment and then asked him how far back this stand went. A shrug, was the answer. I paused again and, finally, I asked if he'd ever dreamed of doing anything different. No, was the answer.

I shared with him that I was in the process of trying to figure out what to do with my life—and that sort of questioning was almost a rite of passage for people like me back in America. He laughed and explained that in Morocco—or at least, in his Morocco—what to do with life was never a question. You are born into it, and like the root of a tree extending through the soil of time, your purpose is to continue its push through the layers of each age. In such a way, the contours may change with each generation's unique conditions, but the purpose it grows from and the meaning it seeks always remain the same. I smiled.

It would be trite to call that a job or a career. It was something more fundamental, more archetypal. This was not a minimum wage job at a grocery store; this was a man who dealt in flavors. To stand and talk with me was as much a fulfillment of his duties as was the sourcing of his spices, the pricing of them, and the displaying of them.

As I continued my travels through the colorful culture of Morocco, I could see this tradition reflected in the landscape itself. Mountainside villages constructed entirely of clay pulled from the earth, with newly molded dwellings built on top of crumbled-out foundations of the same design. They appeared identical to the way they were hundreds, even thousands, of years earlier. Same village, same clay, same architecture—different humans.

If I saw anything modern, its presentation was still shaped by the tradition to which its purpose had to serve. At one point, we were taken over mountains by a driver in an economy van. At another, by a driver on camelback. Same vocation, different tools. I encountered more and more living vocation of all types represented in my generational contemporaries. Each of them showed me how purpose is less about the work we do and more about the roots we nourish to keep a larger garden of life alive. Shepherds who know the secret of the mountains. Farmers who pull treasures from the fields. Innkeepers who hold spaces for others. Builders who create them. Guides who weave us through it all.

It wasn't long until I came across a tradition that touched my heart in a way I'm only just now coming to understand: *the storyteller.* In Morocco, storytellers walk through the markets like living encyclopedias on two feet, carrying with them age-old tales passed on to inspire and intrigue. For travelers like me, visiting from all across the world, these stories are a primary export from an oasis in the desert where people have long come together. They are like trinkets to take back home and remember how stepping foot on that desert oasis soil moved you and could perhaps move those you bring it home to as well.

Stories truly are Morocco's export. Being the birthplace of tales captured in the compendium sold as a book known as *One Thousand and One Arabian Nights* alludes to the sheer volume of tales the culture has made. Film studios hidden in the Sahara desert and Atlas Mountains have put stories like *Gladiator* and *Game of Thrones* on screens the world over. It is, and has been for generations, a true marketplace of stories born from the deep roots of makers and mystics.

In the Moroccan storyteller tradition, when a traveler is walking through a bustling marketplace like Marrakesh, the storyteller will size up this customer and determine the right story for them to hear at that place and time. The hope is that your fortune and their talent conspire in your favor, and as a customer, you are given something that will be precious to you, and perhaps only you. It is like looking for a crystal in a magical shop that speaks expressly to you. It's said that all of us have a story that winds perfectly around our soul and that we will know it in our hearts when we find it. To be given such a story is to be given something precious. We all have one out there, but we must find it. For when you do, you also find your life's meaning—and through retelling it yourself as you grow older, you may begin to unfold your purpose.

The story I found on that trip is called "The Water of Paradise." To me, it carries a deep lesson about what it means to be the keeper of the ground you rest upon, whatever you inherit from it. To you, it may mean something different. Originally attributed to the reign of Harun al-Rashid, a historical figure, the fifth caliph of the Abbasid dynasty in Iraq, it is an old folktale that traveled far to land in Morocco's marketplace of stories. Whether true or not, its roots, hardy from their desert beginnings, have spread across generations and continents of telling and retelling, taking on the magical glimmer of myth nourishing whatever cultural soil it touches with its teachings. My retelling of it goes like this:

Long ago, there was a great ruler, a caliph, of a flourishing desert empire. He was admired for his keen mind, poetic heart, and his power. Most of all, he was renowned for his wise diplomacy. He kept a close adviser at his side who gave him careful guidance on every decision he made for the empire. It is said that he, the adviser, was the first to greet the shepherd who arrived one night, breathless and excited. The shepherd had traveled for many days and many nights, leaving his flock behind in the care of his family so he could urgently bring with him an extraordinary gift directly to the caliph.

The guards at the gates had walked him into the palace grounds after his relentless pleading. But when the adviser finally came down to greet him, the shepherd was speechless, gazing in awe at the majesty and splendor of the place. Ragged and covered in dirt, he was an unusual vision to see in such a place.

"What are you doing here?" the adviser shot to the shepherd, snapping him out of his silent awe.

The shepherd turned his eyes to meet the adviser's gaze. "I've come to see the caliph," he said with soft conviction.

The adviser, holding back laughter, smiled. "The caliph is a very busy man. He has no time for beggars. Now, be gone!"

Unrelenting, the shepherd insisted, "No, please, you must listen. I have discovered something precious. I have brought it all this way as a gift for the caliph. He must see what I have come to bring!" With that, he held out a waterskin bag, as dirty a vision as him.

The adviser, unable to keep his laughter within, let out a howl and then a sigh before asking, "What could possibly be so precious inside such a skin?"

In a rush of words, the shepherd explained, "I was crossing the desert to the south with my flock when I came upon an amazing sight. It was one of my sheep that led the way. She was licking at the sand. I didn't know why, but I was curious what would cause her to do such a thing, so I started digging—"

"And you found?" the adviser interrupted.

"A spring! Underneath the desert sands, I found a spring. Water in the middle of endless dry sand as far as the eye could see. It's a miracle!" To the shepherd, accustomed to a nomadic lifestyle across the vast desert landscape, water was more precious than diamonds or gold. To the adviser, living among the comforts of the palace, water was a trivial everyday thing.

"Why does this matter to the caliph?" the adviser narrowed his eyes and asked.

"Sir." The shepherd bowed deferentially. "When I tasted this water, never in my life have I experienced anything so nourishing

or a flavor so delicious. It is better than anything I could have ever dreamed. A true treasure for which it could only be my duty to bring to the great caliph himself immediately."

"Do you think the caliph has not tasted water?" the adviser challenged.

"Sir, I am a simple man. I know nothing of luxury, but my father and his father and his father passed down stories of the 'Water of Paradise' to me. To them, it was only legend and now I am the one who has found it. I must offer it to the caliph."

The adviser, seeing the earnestness in the shepherd's eyes, relented and walked him to meet the great caliph. When the shepherd shared his urgent news with the caliph, he called for his golden cup, bejeweled with precious stones that reflected the resplendent colors of his great empire. He instructed the shepherd to pour some water into the cup and share it with a bodyguard who would be the first to drink it. As he took a sip, the room filled with a loaded silence as the shepherd, the adviser, the caliph, and his servants all watched the bodyguard. He nodded to the caliph to assure its safety. Walking over to the caliph, he handed over the golden cup and the caliph held it to his lips, curiously sniffed it, and took a sip. The room fell silent. Not a breath as the caliph considered the taste. The shepherd closed his eyes and reveled in the moment. This was the day when his family delivered the Water of Paradise to Harun al-Rashid, the Ruler of Day and Night, keeper of their great empire, and it was he who made it happen.

The caliph only nodded quietly in deep consideration without speaking.

"Should we put him to death?" the adviser broke the silence and asked.

"No. No, of course not," the caliph whispered, still in the quiet of his thinking. Turning to face the shepherd directly, the caliph spoke. "You are a good man. I want to thank you for bringing me such a precious gift." As the shepherd melted in joy, the caliph turned to the *adviser and bodyguards, whispering, "Before the sun rises, escort him out of the palace by the path he came. Do not let him see the rushing of the Tigris River. Do not let him taste the clean water we enjoy and yet find so ordinary. Return him to his desert and escort him back to his flock. When he arrives at home, present to him a bag of gold and announce to him and his family that he and all of his sons who will follow him shall forever be the guardians of the Water of Paradise."*

When the shepherd arrived home and those words from the great caliph were spoken, his heart filled with pride. To this day, his family remains the guardians of their desert spring, firm in their belief that they look after the Water of Paradise as the great caliph said it must be.

Every culture has its stories. Some come from history, some come from fantasies, some come from somewhere in between. Fairy tales, folk stories, legends, myths, movies, dreams. Their power is measured in how we honor them. No matter your station in life and what luxuries you may or may not have, a story given is precious to receive. To taste it deeply, you must understand not just how it sits in you, but what it means to the hands that bring it. The story about the story, the taste of the soil of the culture that offers you its flavor of life.

A Journey

Soil of Your Life

A journey brings experience.

Every year's cycle brings its harvest of meaning from the soil of a culture's stories. Across many cultures' folk traditions is the act of gathering in a circle to share what each individual's experiences brings. It's a coming together to see how the hard facts of experience have changed.

During the pandemic lockdowns of 2020, I saw many of these gatherings come online. Indigenous peoples all across the planet that had planned to gather at the United Nations for a summit were forced to connect digitally over video. The benefit to the world of that was in how it prompted them to share their gathering in an accessible public forum that people like me could tune in live to watch, listen, and learn from deeply— deeply grounded perspectives from the Pacific Islands, northern Europe, the Americas, Africa, and others sharing council in this earth-shaking moment on our planet. These were voices I, as a modern American digital native immersed in social media's fast-moving conversations, had not encountered in such a stark way.

There was a structure to how they initiated the gathering. Every person around the circle would introduce themselves by stating their name, their tribe, and their teaching. That teaching was like the creative magic they were in the unique charge of carrying. It could take many forms. For some, that teaching was the magic of song or prayer. For others, it was activism or a generational perspective. Some were keepers of seeds and keepers of stories, which carried a specific wisdom they would offer to the circle. Whatever it was, it was their unique contribution to the circle that clearly and profoundly arose from what they are made of; what they rest upon. It was like bringing a handful of the soil of their life to drop into the center of a circle at the heart of the world.

When things seem to be falling apart, it's the deeper layers of cultural soil that become the foundation you can rely on to make sense of things. Older ways that have shown their sturdiness against the seismic shifts that shake loose what is younger and new. With a mug of freshly brewed coffee in my hand, I sat on the floor in front of my couch in the morning light of my downtown Los Angeles apartment watching this global digital gathering on my television screen. I broke from the sound of whirring helicopters echoing over the concrete buildings outside my window where the restlessness of 2020's protests still stirred and I fell into my curiosity about what I was watching. What would I say if I were to enter this circle? What is my community? What is my teaching? What soil would the journeys of my life bring to such a gathering?

That is a question worth asking. What would you bring into a circle that asked you to share the soil of your life? Everyone has a story, but not all of us know how to tell it. In the same way, everyone has the creative spark, but not all of us know how to find it. It begins with understanding what you're made of. We all rest upon a story; we just might not be living it. Put another way, as a creative professional, I've hired dozens of people and have built a few teams. I've opened every interview I've ever conducted with some version of the same request: *tell me your story*. It's not about what you say, it's about how. That's where the magic, the creative power, really is. So tell me . . . what are you made of? What is your story?

What is your name?
What is the name you were born with? Why was it given to you?
What is your family name? What does it mean?
What are the nicknames your friends call you by? How did you get them?
What are the names of your avatars in other spaces? Why did you choose them?
What totems do you identify with? How did you find them?

What is your community?
What is your hometown? Are you still connected with it?
What is your city? Did you choose it? Why?
What is your school or alma mater? What brought you there? What did you learn?
What is your company? With whom do you spend most of your time in work or play?
What are the affiliations most pronounced for your identity? Did you choose them?

What is your teaching?
What can you do that few or no one else can like you?
What do you believe that others don't?
What is your mission and vision to achieve it?
What gifts have been given to you?
What truth do you carry?

How much more interesting are all of these questions than the networking classic "What do you do?" Each of them is the key to a door you can open that unlocks a vista of deeper histories. If you find yourself staring at the challenge of a blank canvas, a blank page, or blinking cursor, look down. Start with where you are and what you're made of. You are made of so much more than you might think. You carry an estimated thirty trillion cells vibrating together to make up your being. Binding them together is the story that made you. What will you make with it?

A Lesson

Badass Grounding

A lesson plants a seed.

It was the tail end of a retreat and I was on quite the ego trip. I was charged up and impressed with myself for the breakthroughs I'd had among this community of great thinkers, doers, open hearts, and people unafraid to share their dreams. We had sat in a circle and shared our experiences one by one of the trials and tribulations that weekend had brought for each of us. Our triumphs, our failures, but most of all our lessons and the awakening of our personal creative magic that had opened for us each in between. Nobody knew what anybody "did" as far as professional life goes, but we understood each other deeply. We had seen how we'd shown up for ourselves and for each other.

After the session closed, we began to disperse around the gardens of the property for some quiet reflection. I was idly swinging back and forth on a wooden two-person swinging bench overlooking a birdbath with my notebook in my lap. I was brimming with energy, excited for how I would bring my breakthroughs out to the people around me. My train of self-aggrandizing fantasies was halted when I heard a voice.

"Is it okay if I sit with you?" a woman's voice tenderly asked.

I squinted up from the pages of my notebook at her standing over me in the morning light. She appeared first as a shadow until my eyes adjusted to the comforting earth tones of the patterned blanket she had wrapped around her shoulders to guard herself from the crisp air. I nodded and gestured to the space next to me on the swing.

We sat together for a moment in a shared contemplative silence that she soon broke. "That was quite something you shared in there." I nodded again. "It made me think a lot about the kind of people who lead. It made me think of the difference between the most powerful leaders and the ones who give themselves the title of something like *shaman* or *medicine man* or, screw it, any kind of word that implies that they're in any way responsible for a group of people's journey. Even if they aren't ready."

I raised an eyebrow, kept looking straight ahead, playing with a soft river stone underneath my toe in front of the bench.

"Do you know what the real ones have going on?" she continued. I shook my head. "Bad. Ass. Grounding." She emphasized each word. I chuckled.

"Badass grounding?" I parroted back.

"Badass grounding. It's not about putting on your show. It's about holding it down for other people's journeys. The great ones . . . their presence is so *unbelievably heavy* that you might not even know they are there, but you would know that you feel safe when you're around them when they're doing their thing. The show goes on for everyone else. They hold it down so everyone else can get charged up. When everyone knows they've got the heavy in their corner, that's when it gets wild in the best way. Without someone to hold it down, it's no good. People get lost. People get crazy. The bigger the work, the heavier the grounding. You get what I'm saying?" I turned to see her locking me square in the eyes. Her presence was heavy. In the depth of her stare, I understood. I nodded silently.

A lot of people want to fly, but it's the people who hold it down that make the greatest leaps possible. Give thanks to the ground's keepers. When you don't know what to do, look down and thank the ground you rest upon and whoever might have been keeping it for you. Start with where you are, then you will see where you're going.

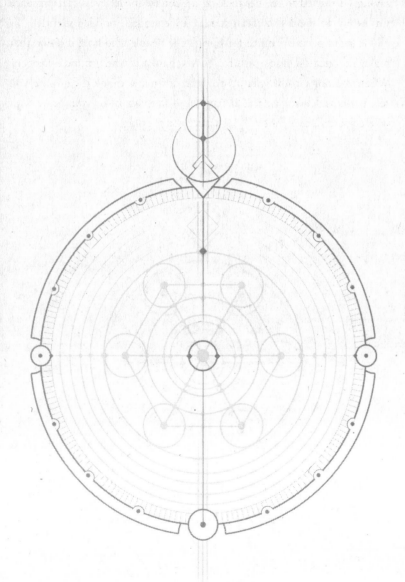

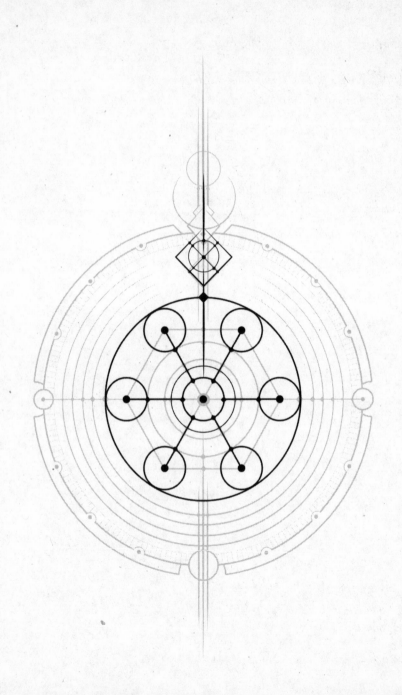

●

A Point

North Stars Change

A point starts somewhere.

Look up. What you call your ceiling today will tomorrow become your floor. Look up even farther and see the height of your aspirations. Life keeps climbing. That's what we do. We reach for the light above that shines with an unknowable mystery we could never fully grasp, no matter how clearly we see. The sky has no horizon. The journey toward the light is never complete. Your life, your dreams, your ideas of truth are but paint on the mausoleum ceiling of your beliefs.

Keep reaching and you will keep breaking through to a higher, clearer, and more brilliant shine. Whether the sun, the moon, the planets, or the constellations in the sky, the lights we are drawn to change. Aspiration is an adaptation of evolution. The world keeps turning and North Stars change.

It is a fact that there is no true North Star. While many think of *the* North Star as being a fixed point in the sky, every thirteen thousand years the earth's North Star changes, switching between the star Polaris we use today and the star Vega that seems nearly on the other side of the sky. Even the Earth's magnetic poles are known to flip. How different must human imagination be when something so fundamental as the North Star changes? Which way is north? It depends who you are asking and when.

The way the light hits us is always changing. As the stars in the sky drift overhead, different stars and different constellations cast their shine to inspire their different stories of what to reach toward. If all the world's a stage, then the lights above set the scenes for it, coloring the characters and settings for how we play.

How does the light shine on you? What is your spotlight? What is your stage? That is the charge of inspiration that the direction of "what shines upon you" gives. If the soil holds your character, the sky casts your play. Every moment moves through the cycles of what shines upon you in the ceaseless unfolding of your story. Look up. What is the light telling you today?

A Vision

The Revolution
Keeps on Turning

A vision inspires action.

Light has a charge. It colors the moment for every season with a unique shine that defines it. Moments can be the flash of an instant, they can be the glow of an age, and so much else in between. There are many ways to slice time, but it's always changes in the light that do the cutting. Change is the only constant.

Everything is in motion always. Nature moves in cycles. The world is always turning as the sun, the moon, and the stars are always turning with it. The best we can do is to measure the movement of the changes in the light to understand where we are in this moment of nature's dancing cosmic play.

The revolution is always turning. Seasons change, shifting stories with them. Seasons cycle continuously. Moments only come once. A moment is what makes this time special in a season's cycle of repeating. The color of the year, the latest fashion trend, the breakthrough

technology, dance-floor beat, or pressing issue; the new heroes and villains of culture's story keep turning round and round. The shared creative
vision of collective culture turns with the shifts in the light. Just as each
coming spring becomes a time for planting new seeds and each approaching fall has us take stock of all we've harvested, the turning of the wheel
of the light guides what is, simply put, in fashion versus what is boring.

There's a difference between chasing a season's trend and dancing
with a moment's movements. When you're chasing, you're trying to keep
up with the change. When you're dancing, you're in the groove of the
music of the spheres. One eye on the dance floor and the other on the
rising dawn of a new light cast on the next exciting scene. For a maker,
a marketer, or a mystic—a creator in any way—stillness is death. It can
be an insatiable desire to see your story play out onstage. Or, at the very
least, to be among those in the crowd who understand it. Even simply
having a vision of where the light is shining gives you a chance to catch
the moment's grace.

There is an ordering underneath the changes that can help you to
see where the light is headed. Follow the sun. Literally. It's as simple as
the seasons. The warmth of summer, the cool of winter. The transforma-
tions of fall and spring. Human culture responds to the reliable tides of
these seasons just as the rest of nature does. Budding romances and fresh
ideas alongside the blooming of flowers in spring, the stowing away to
our homey retreats in the winter alongside the gathering of seeds and
hibernating animals in their dens. Holidays drawn on the cycle's calen-
dar mark the moments of transition with ritual. Some are sacred like the
rites of spring, some secular like back to school, but each is rooted in the
natural cycles of light's change just the same. These ebbs and flows to culture and life come from the literal shifts in how the light hits us. Cycles
borne out of the tilt of the earth as it takes its journey around the sun,
altering the vibrancy and hue of the light of the sun and stars as we see it.
Creeping darkness. Growing light. Shifting hues in the creative vision we
all share together to understand our shifting story through the change.

The world of products and fashion releases new colors, styles, ways of moving, and exchanging currency that follow seasons marked with the turning of the solar year. The 365 days it takes for Earth to complete its journey around the sun that gives us spring, summer, fall, and winter. The four quarters of the fiscal year. Like the four beats of a musical measure, industry and culture groove to the rhythm of those key days in the year that announce the release of each new idea against the great shared creative vision. "This is the year of *blank*," the culture's vision keepers reliably proclaim. Theme, trend, provocation, whatever you call it, it's a description of the season and a commitment to a role in the play. It's all a show, and we're all in it together, even as we try to stand apart.

Nostalgia is a mechanism of reliable proof for how longer cycles play. Generational blocks of ten, twenty, or a hundred years and longer provide more subtle returns, and push things out of fashion and then pull them right back in again. The older among us smile with dismissive déjà vu as the young parade around new ideas they think are fresh to them. Reboot. Remake. Been there, loved that. Maybe didn't need to see it again. There's a steady rhythm to the human psyche as our emotions turn through cultures that grace the global stage. There's an art to it that is not a science. It's a matter of correlative cycles through feelings more than causal changes in facts. The ancient timekeepers had systems to keep track. They affixed these cycles to the movements of the great clock of the lights in the sky. The planets, which reflect the sun's shine as they drift, cross, and combine above us in the night sky, cast patterns that light the stage of the everlasting human drama. They cause change no more than the hands of a clock push the passage of time, but they keep track of it just the same.

That we have a clockwork shift in lights in the sky to look to at all is utterly fascinating. There are so many who argue about the supposed conflicting views between astronomy, astrology, and astrophysics and what each has to say about the lights in the sky, but they each invite the same basic thing. Look at them. Step outside and look at the lights and see how they make you feel. Whether by the facts of their physics or the grace of their shine, they are a source of inspiration for you to drop deeply into the essence of the seasons. It will never shine on you again the same way as it does right now in this moment. Is that not worth noticing?

At the precipice of the modern age, the astronomers Titius and Bode developed a formula that predicts the placements between planets in not just our, but any given solar system. It was with this formula that the location of distant planets like Uranus and the dwarf planet Ceres was discovered. The implication is intriguing. It implies that while the planets can be known as objects of matter floating in distant space, they can also be understood as points of resonance in a field where the matter that makes up those planets *should* be according to the music of the spheres. A gathering of dust around a star condenses into a planetary system according to an unseen blueprint underneath. Regardless of what the movements of the planets may or may not cause, their presence is the effect of a deeper pattern. Stuff and story. Matter and meaning. Every solar system is a clock counting the beats to the movements for whatever life it keeps. The drama of creation ceaselessly unfolds through its cycles, and even our most audacious ideas are but brief moments within its seasons.

The makers and the marketers look to the short cycles of trends and fashion. The mystics look to the broader and more sweeping cycles of change. They each understand the same thing: change is the only constant. The human story evolves substantially across the slow-moving, but certain, turning of the wheel of the planets and stars. Everything we believe and the systems we use to believe it can change. The same mechanism of Earth's movement that turns the night sky between two different North Stars every thirteen thousand years also turns the wheel of the great ages of the zodiac, shifting ever so slightly how the earth receives the light of the sun and perhaps altering the very character of our seasons and the climate of our continents. The ancient timekeepers kept track carefully. Temples built to match the shapes of constellations in the sky point due east toward precisely where the sun rises on the first day of spring's equinox. Every year, that rising constellation that shines with the sun strikes like twelve o'clock to announce what time it is at the scale of a cosmic age. Slowly, across every 2,500 years or so, that constellation changes. These are the hours that track the great seasons of humanity's grandest stories. We call them the "great ages," or the zodiac.

Each of those seasons we call the great ages were minted with a zodiac symbol that holds the characters and plot of each age's story, like the synopsis to a play. Each holds the infusion of feelings that drive human ambitions toward a new creative vision of heroes, villains, ambitions, fashions, sights, sounds, and inventions as told by where the light will start to shine in our shared sky. New spotlights, new shadows, new stories, new cultures for each newly passing age.

Looking back to the horizon of where archeology has written the beginnings of the human story, we can correlate each age's symbolic meaning to get a glimpse at not only what humanity's past cycle of cultural trends and beliefs could have been, but also how profoundly they can evolve beyond today's. The proofs are in the records. As a storytelling model for segmenting history, the correlations are striking. We can see in the available facts an implication of feelings about where humanity reached for which light and when. The cycle of human history is a story of all of these ages, seasons, and hours through which our collective true north has changed. Even our most deeply held beliefs can change as easily as turning toward a new set of stars in the sky to shine down their meaning.

To the materialist, the zodiac is nothing. To the mystic, the zodiac is an index of human beliefs. To the marketer, an encyclopedia of stories. Make of it what you will, but consider the warmth within the implication of our inheritance of these vessels of meaning older than time. Whatever story we are going through now, no matter how challenging or rife with uncertainty, perhaps we have been through it together before in some way. We are only navigating the peculiarities of our moment in the vast, turning wheel of fast cycles within slow cycles to the human story's seasons. We are playing with the music of the spheres. As a wise music teacher once taught me, you can't really play the music fast until you understand how to play it slow.

Twelve thousand years ago, humanity was sheltering from a darkness of some kind. Perhaps it was an Ice Age driven by some geological shift or sudden calamity. The mystics call this the Age of Cancer, branded with the symbol of the self-sheltering hard-shelled crab. Our true north was in the warm fire of the hearth. We sought the light of nurturing protection and retreated from the shadow of winter's biting fangs.

Then came the Age of Gemini, branded with the symbol of the dancing, conversing twins. Our true north was emergence from the dimness of our dens into the light of the market and the thrill of discovering the others and the inventions, skills, and performances they bring. A true north reaching for the power of words in language, innovation, and trade.

Then came the Age of Taurus, branded with the symbol of the earth-shaping bull. All of our play together needed rules. Our true north became boundaries established for the common good. This was a time of the establishment of empires on the grounds of these markets, the harnessing of herding and agriculture to draw lines in the sand and build. The heroic power of the oxen and cattle to till the soil and the need for orderly rule speak in the symbol and worship of Taurus's bull, the living embodiment of ingenuity in the light of this next true north. This was the time of the first great kingdoms of Mesopotamia and Mesoamerica, the cradles of civilization.

Then came the Age of Aries, branded with the symbol of the boastful ram. A rising true north suggested heroism in testing the rules, if not breaking them. The light of heroism turned to those who do it best, our champions. Here we saw the rise of the Olympic Games, celebrating champions of sport, art, and philosophy. We saw the rise of great conquerors who stood proudly on mountains of achievement in glorious light like the battle-worn, victorious ram. Alexander the Great. Genghis Khan. Cyrus of Persia. Blood on the shining armor of their breastplates, these rule-breakers and -makers embodied both hero and villain depending on where you stand.

The brutality of champions and their need for wars brought about the Age of Pisces, branded with the symbol of two fish, locked in eternal opposition—polarization, separation. One above water, one below. Our true north became the notion that we were lost, needing to be found. This was a time for the enlightened ones. Jesus, Buddha, Muhammad, Isaac Newton, Copernicus, Galileo, and Darwin, among others, whose heroic revelations promised to shine a light of certainty out of the darkness of the uncertain. In the age of separation, each way to the light defined itself also in opposition of the others. Which way is north in the age of the separated fishes became a fundamental argument of reality's very perception. The heroes in this age's story are nothing without their villains.

Today, we are in a transition between two great seasons. The sun of the Age of Pisces is setting and the sun of the Age of Aquarius is at its rise. The story of polarity, opposites, is losing its exaltation, loosening its grip on our imaginations. The time of a planet separated by its poles in conquest of each other is giving way to a rising vision of a global tribe. Each new generation born is one step closer to the story ahead and one step farther away from the one behind. The dramatic tension between age groups hits culture like a software upgrade embodied in the hardware of new humans. The creative visions expressing the piscine dream are resented. Anti-religion, anti-science, anti-everything polarization are characters cloaked in shadow, feeling flat and boring, even hostile or backward to the young. As the revolution keeps on turning, the light is always shining onward toward newer dreams.

The old true north of individuation, survival of the fittest, and opposition of gender, politics, religion, anything related to identity, is giving way to the next true north of non-binaries, fluidity, and mutualistic community aid. To the old, it's chaotic. To the young, it makes perfect sense. It's the blueprint underneath which the most macro of trends guides the change. The resonant points have shifted. There's a new story that wants to happen. We're not a fish out of water; we're in it.

This is the Age of Aquarius, branded with the symbol of the cupbearer who holds the water that keeps us connected and knows the importance of keeping it clean. This symbol, appropriate for the times, is rich with the complexity of myth. It tells of the young prince Ganymede, known for his beauty and who was discovered by Zeus in a field, who swept down as an eagle and whisked him away to be cupbearer to the gods. There are layers upon layers to the story of who the cupbearer is and what happened to them, each detail imbued with profound meaning. What is a field? What is beauty? What is it to discover and be discovered by a higher being? That itself is a part of this age's illumination. Within this new true north is the invitation to unlock the secrets buried within our myths. The myths themselves are like the feeling-bearing elixirs you hold in your cup, into which you can see your reflection and experience its taste. It's a time of learning that you are responsible for the stories you hold and the stories you share.

You control whether what you keep in your cup is medicine or poison, bitter or sweet. This season's true north is realizing that we are all mixed together and have a responsibility for what we collectively keep. We inhale each other's exhales. We hold a shared culture in our communities, feeling the want to cast out and call in what we believe belongs. The light of this true north shines on the connections between things. Inventions like the internet, blockchain, the global economy, communication networks, and discoveries like the quantum field, control measures for the planetary climate and the microbiome emerging in the last century correlate to the rising story of this age. Those ideas have always been there. They used to be unnoticed, unfashionable, unrealized, or boring. It's just that the light started to shine where we could see. How curious that the story captured in the zodiac symbol of Aquarius seems to have been forecasted, already written. Perhaps we have been here before and will be here again.

The revolution doesn't have to be televised. It's always playing in the stars overhead. You just have to look up and see. The revolution keeps on turning; its shifting lights carry the tides of people's beliefs. What you create lives and breathes in the stories within such beliefs. Stories, like the seasons, rise and set like the sun across hours, days, months, years, and centuries. There is no telling exactly when the first colors of each story begin or when they definitively fade. Change is a constant transition. You, as a participant in creation, are underneath the lights of that story. Make your moment in this season's cycle. Look up, appreciate, take notice of the shining dance in the music of the spheres. Find your role to play in the song of this season's true north and join in.

A Compass

Activating: Between Light and Darkness

A compass sets direction.

The direction of "what shines upon you" is about inspiration. It's about how to show up in this moment, whatever it is. Lightning strikes of big ideas, spotlights of opportunity that put you on center stage. The activating energy of what is above you is about how you show up creatively with something exciting in the here and now. Every moment's shine is different. Only the light of the present moment is real. How it hits you now colors the story by which you see the past and the future.

For the trend casters, future tellers, and vision keepers of the world, what is above you is about connecting with the great story in the sky told in the constant dance of light and darkness that moves the human imagination. What are the great dramas unfolding and who are its cast of characters? What is the story that wants to be told through the shapes and the colors cast by this moment's light? Close your eyes and connect, not just with what you see, but what you don't. The story of a moment is

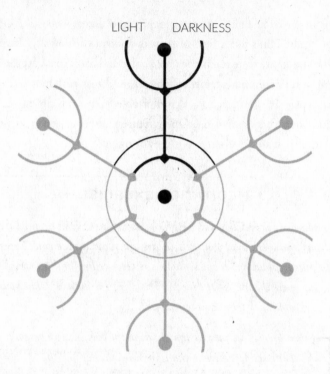

LIGHT   DARKNESS

written not just by what is there, but also by what wants to be but isn't. This is the interplay of light and darkness, the seen and the unseen.

Tuning in meditatively, searching for inspiration in your creative vision, light, the seen, is the attractive energy, whereas dark, the unseen, is the repulsive. These two poles have long been the subject of deep consideration in the human imagination, mythologized into notions of good and evil. The anxieties of those mythologies are rich with creative charge, offering diametric inspiration into your creative vision from above. The darkness of the unseen is pregnant with possibility, enticing your imagination to fill its empty spaces, and challenging the accepted story of the way things are. That is, after all, the exalted role every villain plays. They are the source of questioning, the unseen driver that moves the turning wheel of light. Revolution. The light of the seen is a guiding principle, granting insight in return for your praise. Cowering against shadow and lifting toward the light, human imagination across collective culture withers and blooms like a field of flowers under a turning sky. Together, shadow and light create the intricacy of color and form that cast the story for you to act upon in movement with seasons across each moment's invitation to play. Find a place to get comfortable, prepare to close your eyes, and tune into this meditation. Open yourself up to whatever surprising inspiration that shines upon you might bring.

◆ MEDITATION EXERCISE ◆

*When you are ready, close your eyes and breathe in light from above into your heart and then, with your exhale, breathe it out **above you**. Experience within your imagination what is above whatever ceiling and into the sky. Do you know where the sun is? The moon? The stars? The planets? Close your eyes, go in, and come back when you're ready.*

On your next breath, see in your imagination the opening of a gateway above you, only about six feet higher than your head. Beyond this gate are the answers to the question "What shines upon you?" Once you go in, take your time and breathe through as many cycles as you want to notice the thoughts, feelings, and experiences that arise in response to that question.

There are no coincidences when you ask the question and move through the gate. Take your time and experience them. If it feels like nothing is happening, you can always breathe out and ask the question again and breathe in to see what replies. When you are ready, close your eyes and go in. What shines upon you? Come back when you are ready. ◆

A Star

A Love Letter to the Stars

A star lights the way.

I've long looked up at the sky and wondered. At a young age, I was entranced by astronomy. I remember the warm, peculiar smile the librarians would give me as I, at the green age of ten, would check out books about astrophysics. Kids have a way of sucking up all the information they can find about what activates them. It becomes their "thing" that patterns their pajamas, bedsheets, and birthday cakes. Space was my thing. By the grace of my parents' support, I got to live a little astronomy nerd's dream and go to Space Camp. This was the kind of prize I saw them give to winners on television game shows, and I got to experience it as a real-life thing.

At Space Camp, we met the astronauts we wanted to someday be like, and we were given our own special roles in a pretend space shuttle mission, for which we went through a whole gamut of pretend training. We learned the science behind rockets that stood taller than skyscrapers when we saw them in person. We peered into NASA's mission control center, and we learned the details behind all of the great space missions that great minds and brave hearts had accomplished before. There, Apollo was the namesake of the missions that reached for the sky and landed on the moon. Feats of vision and accuracy achieved by the wonders of engineering. As mighty as the Saturn V rocket stood or as penetrating as the images from the Hubble telescope made me feel, it was the story of the Voyager mission that affected me the most.

What first drew me to the Voyager mission was how sophisticated their planning and timing was. It was like throwing a couple of stones into the sky at just the right moment so that they could dance across the whole of our solar system, kissing each of the shining planets along the way. Launched at precisely the right moment in the turning of Earth and other planets around the sun, with a programmed sequence of just the right propulsion, *Voyager 1* and *Voyager 2*, like stars themselves, journeyed into the cosmos farther than anything human made (to our knowledge) ever had, sending back photos along the way. These were the photos of the planets plastered on my classroom walls that had enchanted me with space in the first place.

As I grew older, the story of the *Voyagers* grew with me, and I came to learn more layers of what those stars we put in the sky really meant. To this day, the *Voyagers* are still going, getting farther and farther from Earth each moment, 14.6 billion miles and counting. The *Voyagers* carry with them what I consider to be the greatest love story ever told, because it could perhaps someday be the only love story that remains. It is a story of real people. Every year, as the *Voyagers* recede even farther away, their tales become closer to myth.

Carl Sagan was a professor at Cornell University who, through his PhD thesis and published articles on planetary astrophysics, became a close adviser to the NASA space program, helping to shape their missions to explore our solar system. As a gifted communicator to the broader public, Sagan stood tall as both an accomplished scientist and advocate of skeptical scientific inquiry. A recognizable figure in books, television, and popular culture, he famously stated his concern for a future full of superstition and misplaced belief toward what feels good, rather than what is true. He feared a future where people look to crystals and horoscopes for answers rather than deploy knowledge and critical thinking to question those in authority. His concerns ring so prophetically true for the many who look around equipped with the sort of skeptical mind he championed and see a modern culture dumbed down and confused that his character has itself crystallized as its own star—the very archetype of the skeptical scientific mind.

Keeping his skepticism intact, Carl Sagan carried a deep reverence for the unknown. It was from this reverence that he was made chair of the NASA committee to construct a capsule of contents that would journey with the Voyager probes to the far reaches of space. It was a shot at escaping the reaches of our solar system made possible only by a perfect alignment of the planets. In the opportunity to receive messages from the stars, the team behind the mission recognized it was an opportunity to also give a message in return. The committee's task was to attach to the probes whatever might tell the story of life on Earth best for whoever out there might find them in the billions of years the Voyager journeys might last. A love letter to the stars. Communicating as best as we can, "We are here, and we hope you are too."

The committee assembled an elegantly designed system of universally translatable language that would reveal the interstellar coordinates of Earth and instructions on how to access data recorded onto a golden record attached to the side of the Voyager probes. It is a marvel of design-based thinking. The remaining challenge, then, was how to figure out what to put on that record. How do you decide which stories to tell to adequately capture Earth's diversity of life and culture?

Enter Ann Druyan. Ann Druyan was designated as the creative director of the committee behind the Voyager golden record. Her creative task was one of epic curation. Her deep and wide knowledge of artistic mediums and culture afforded her the vision to see, hear, and feel what messages to place in this bottle cast out into the deep. Under her direction, the team wrote onto the golden record the lulling waves of the ocean's tides, the piercing shout of Chuck Berry's electric guitar, swells of indigenous songs, and the symmetric symphonic crescendos of Beethoven and Bach. The orbital velocities of Mercury, Venus, Earth, Mars, and Jupiter were inscribed as vibrations along with the sounds of volcanoes and earthquakes. The night song of frogs, crickets, monkeys, and wolves joined the chorus with the underwater recordings of the music of whales. The sound of a kiss and a mother cooing to her child. Greetings in languages spoken by representatives of the United Nations. Images were encoded in sound, depicting animal forms, the human life cycle, sophisticated architecture, and technological feats.

The assembly of the record was its own journey for the committee. Ann Druyan had been searching endlessly for a suitable Chinese folk song to include, when she came upon a 2,500-year-old song called "Flowing Stream." Excited at the discovery, she called Carl Sagan and left him a voicemail. An hour later, he called her back, and they began a conversation.

The most uncertain portion of the Voyager missions would be when they crossed the line after which they would no longer be in our solar system, entering deep, interstellar space. It's the edge of what is known as the heliosphere. There was no way of knowing what would happen when they reached across the line, but it was certain to be a sudden moment of change after a long, long journey. Carl and Ann passed through a similar line on that phone call. They fell in love. Perhaps they had fallen in love long before, on the journey it took to get to that phone call, but it was on that telephone line that they proclaimed it and decided to get married.

It was a love born from the mythic music they were making together in the creation of the golden record. It was also a love born out of breaking. Carl himself was already married to another member of the committee. Ann, too, was already engaged to another, also on the committee. Every love has its story, full of complexities written by broken bonds and new beginnings. The music of harmony and dissonance. It is a sacred act of creation between feelings in the heart that defy what might make sense to the facts of the mind. Like all creation, love is a struggle. That is its magic. This was a marriage of the certainty of science, the uncertainty of spirit, and the reverence of art to bridge the gap. The grace of humans reaching.

There was something else the golden record needed to carry with it. The music of the human mind, recorded in the electrical impulses of a human brain and nervous system. The hope was that perhaps a sophisticated alien civilization might be able to reverse engineer those sounds back into the thoughts that shaped them and understand what it was to be human from the inside. A whisper across two eternities. The committee just needed to decide which human to record. They chose Ann Druyan. Only days after her fateful phone call with Carl, she sat in a chair connected to wires that committed the sounds of her head, heart, and body to the golden record. As she recounts it, she spent that time in the chair meditating on the wonder of being in love and all the complexity it brings. The beauty. The mess. The humanity. The music of Ann Druyan's heart and the machinations of Carl Sagan's mind, with the support from the body of an unfathomably understanding committee, were etched onto a record made of gold, bolted to the side of a probe in a rocket, and launched into space in 1977 to journey onward for a billion years.

Voyager 1 crossed the line and exited our solar system in 2012. In the time since that mission, Carl Sagan has passed away. Ann Druyan and Timothy Ferris, her prior fiancé and co-committee member, continue to share a story that has since grown to mythic proportions in the imagination of modern culture. They were a group of humans activated by their moment, when the light of all human culture turned upon them. They had to rise to their highest selves to meet it. Not to be perfect, but to be true. Their story lives now forever as the music in the turning of the *Voyagers*, two stars humanity has placed for itself in our sky.

A Journey

Archetypal Creation

A journey brings experience.

The creative journey stretches between the ground of accepting life as it is and the sky of believing in life as it could be. It is how we reach for higher visions of ourselves. Creativity is often regarded as mere ornamentation on the march to human progress. Perhaps it is the drumbeat that drives it.

In 1914, composer Gustav Holst, moved by the great shaking of world war, tried to enlist in the military but was rejected as unfit for service. Resigned to his chair as he lost friends in battle, Holst composed music that moved the world instead. He met his moment by conceiving of an idea to write a symphony dedicated to each of the planets as a way to tell the story through music of the forces that shake the world. The music of the spheres.

It was an enormous creative undertaking, but one that solidified his acclaim. He didn't just look up at the lights in the sky with the inquisitiveness of his mind; he glanced with the curiosity of his heart, letting it build a creative vision for all to experience the music of each planet's theme. Nothing more or less than the act of creation in tribute to how he feels when he beholds each planet's reflection of the light.

His symphonies, entitled *The Planets*, were a triumph in their own time, but Holst's vision has continued to resonate in ways that many do not even realize. The sounds of his symphonies, like an unseen force, continue to play the layers of other creations and other names. Searching for influences for the score of the film *Star Wars*, composer John Williams turned to Holst's planetary symphonies as the basis for his dramatic themes. The dreadful march of Holst's music for Mars became the villainous theme of the militaristic Empire's insatiable thirst for conquest, control, and order. The buoyant swells of Holst's Jupiter symphony informed the uplifting melodic motifs for the film's heroic young Luke Skywalker, seeking his destiny torn between dominion and setting his people free. It was a soundtrack for revolution, the triumph of the human spirit against war. Within the music, borne from the light of the planets, were universal themes that stir the hearts of millions of adoring fans across generations.

Star Wars is a smash success, to say the least. Each of the franchise's many films and series have set consecutive viewership records. Scores of merchandise, video games, and experiences have bolstered the value of the franchise to upwards of $70 billion, enough to nearly qualify itself as its own industry. At its heart is a creative vision that has cemented itself as a pillar of multigenerational storytelling, seared in the collective imagination of enough hearts to regard it as a modern-day myth.

How? Why? Because the layers of creative vision at the heart of Star Wars, like many epic works of generational art, tap feelings that run deep and true: archetypes.

Archetypes are the color wheel of culture. All of our stories are painted with the characters and myths that together we call archetype and within which we relate to universal human truths. The movements of the archetypes in our collective imagination are like the movements of the planets in the sky or the gods and goddesses within our hearts. When we encounter their archetypes in a creation that puts them on mythic display through a film projector's light, we feel the familiarity and our spirits soar in applause. The blockbuster film, most of all, is our modern-day participation in the ritual of connecting with the great vision, the collective story, of our time. Whatever the vehicle of creation, be it film, music, writing, dance, or anything else that might light up your eyes from the glow of a screen, it calls forth from the truer light of an archetypal astral shine. Even if the glowing lights of the city drown out the stars, they are connected to the same story of our evolving human spirit.

I have used archetype as my color palette across many creations. Like color, the combinations of character and story within archetype are infinite. There are numerous systems that break them down into different designs. I have designed artificial intelligence models with tarot cards, I've used gods and goddesses as models for characters in stories, and mood boards for brands. There are many systems you can choose from, and I largely suspect that in the coming age of higher regard for the power of human myths, older and more esoteric systems will be mined by the makers, marketers, and mystics of the world for their power of conveyance in visions that stir the heart and tickle the mind.

As we play with the idea of the lights that shine from above you, it seems appropriate to examine more deeply the archetypal system of the classical planets. These are not the planets as seen by the astronomer's eye, but the planets as seen in the creative vision of the alchemist, the poet, the astral travelers of older times. The great storytellers would use these planets as the blueprints for their characters and stories to great fanfare, as the acclaim of Holst and Star Wars displays.

The classical seven planetary personalities of Western antiquity are arranged not like the scientific ordering of planets. Instead, they are the different layers of the firmament as seen in the sky from the ground of the Earth below. They are, in order: the sun, the moon, Mars, Mercury, Jupiter, Venus, and Saturn.

As the planets move above us, the old vision keepers assigned them personalities to describe the dramas that unfold as they converge, oppose, and square each other in the sky. Those personalities are the archetypes, a word coined by Carl Jung derived from same the Latin root as *architecture* and *archangels*. They are like algorithms in the light, blueprints of human understanding in its most unfiltered, perfected form. The mystics programmed these planetary archetypes with their own vast array of mythologies and correspondences of colors, scents, herbs, animal totems, metals, days of the week, and more. They are like the nine muses of human inspiration, nothing more than the stuff of story, existent only in the kaleidoscopic inner world of imagined meaning. What would you create with them? How would you weave them into your stories?

The Sun Plays the Savior

Sunday is its day. Its archetype is the creative light of clearing with a sanctifying energy that drives out the darkness. The sun holds the foundation of the Greek gods Helios and Apollo, inspiring characters like DC Comics' Superman as well as other core heroes whose journey is at the center of stories and myth about the salvation of all. What else does the sun do each morning but "save the day"?

The Moon Plays the Priestess

Monday is its day. Its archetype is the creative light of intuition. A nurturing energy that conspires toward the evolution of all life, without fear of the darkness. The moon holds the foundation for the Greek goddesses Selene, Artemis, and Hecate, inspiring characters like J. R. R. Tolkien's Galadriel and other powerful priestess characters who are as distinctly forceful as they are beautiful. The cycles of the moon are, after all, at the center of magic and the creative power of the womb.

Mars Plays the Conqueror

Tuesday is its day. Its archetype is the creative light of competition and achievement. A warrior energy that fuels the pride of champions and the violence of tyrants equally. Mars holds the foundation for the Greek god Ares, whose love of war inspires characters like Darth Vader of Star Wars, who play the villain with a complexity that calls for redemption. How interesting that we see the barren landscape of Mars as a landscape we could replenish to host life as we hope it may have once before.

Mercury Plays the Magician

Wednesday is its day. Its archetype is the creative light of innovation, communication, and inventiveness. The character of the magician and the entrepreneur. Mercury holds the foundation for the Greek god Hermes, inspiring quick-witted characters of inventiveness like Marvel's Tony Stark. Fitting that the planet is a big ball of iron that whips quickly around the sun, which it orbits ambitiously close.

Jupiter Plays the King

Thursday is its day. Its archetype is the creative light of ascending sovereignty with the glad joviality of dominion over empires. Jupiter holds the foundation for the Greek god Zeus and Norse god Thor, inspiring rising patriarchal characters like *The Lion King*'s Simba whose story reverberates with the reminder that the crowns of kings are passed on from one generation to the next. There's something wondrous to behold in the majesty of Jupiter's system of eighty moons or more. It seemingly acts like the solar system's benevolent second king to the sun, protecting the inner planets like Earth from the dangers of asteroids and comets by virtue of its gravitational pull, which steers them away. Life may not exist on Earth without it.

Venus Plays the Beauty

Friday is its day. Its archetype is the creative light of love, beauty, and attraction. Venus holds the foundation for the Greek goddess Aphrodite, inspiring a host of beloved characters that have become the object of a culture's collective desire, like the persona of Marilyn Monroe. Of all the planetary lights in the sky, Venus shines the brightest. She is the other to Earth, an inner planet so close yet so far and perhaps, like us, a cradle to life.

Saturn Plays the Dread

Saturday is its day. Its archetype is the creative light of dogma, the cold inevitability of time and expectations of tradition. Saturn is the foundation for the Greek god Kronos, the unyielding father to Zeus who would sooner eat his children than give up his reign. There is a cold villainy in this planetary personality that has inspired characters like Harry Potter's Voldemort, whose chilling name comes as a reminder of a more ancient darkness. To the eyes of antiquity, Saturn was the farthest planet people could see. It represented the very edge of our solar system and perhaps the edge of weight and measure of the matter that gathered around the sun to become the planets that bear us. Like Jupiter with over eighty moons, Saturn lurks in the deep like an old emperor of the dark.

This is just one system of seven archetypes for you to remix and recapitulate among a multitude of colors and forms for you to draw with in your creative visions. There are 5,040 possible combinations of seven numbers. That is 5,040 possible renderings of archetype into character for you to use. How might they eclipse each other? How might they oppose or square off? How might they combine together into one character or a team?

The visions we keep are ultimately tricks of the light. Stories are told by the dance of shadows between the seen and the unseen across human imaginations, like the flicker of flames on the wall or the humming wheel of a projector spinning stories in front of a bulb. Without the vision keepers to channel the stories, perhaps we'd get lost in the light. Old archetypal systems like the planets, the zodiac, the tarot, and others could be mistaken for useless when evaluated by scientific needs. They are tools for the artist. Technology of the spirit, to train the mind and open the heart to look into the light and share what you see. Don't take it from me. Look for yourself.

A Lesson

A Sun Without Planets
Is Only a Star

A lesson plants a seed.

The light shines on us all, but it reaches everyone in a different way. Creativity and vision, these are matters of belief. Nobody could see what you see, feel what you feel, or do what you do with it. There is nothing about your inner world you could prove. That's the play of it. We all play different characters, but we are all shined upon by the same light of the same story. Everyone lives through the uniqueness of their own experience within it.

The direction of "what shines upon you" is about your relationship with the light of each moment and the activating inspiration it brings. Why you and why now? What is your unique contribution to the great play of creation? The spotlights of life are about seeing and being seen for how you see. Reflection. For the creator, their moment of greatness is their moment when they can point others toward the colors and shapes they see in the light that shines upon them. Perhaps you want to be a star.

Perhaps you want to be seen. How would others benefit from it? What is it you believe that would brighten others' skies if you could show them the secrets you see in the shine?

A sun without planets is only a star. Without others to reflect it, its light is lost to the void. A solar system is a blueprint for creation, a model for how to shine together instead of shining alone. Light is only seen when it's shared. Creation is an act of service. The mystics who see visions, the makers who shape them, and the marketers who bring them to the world are the assembly line of inspiration into action into being to make a moment matter. It's those who watch the rising sun every morning and the stars that rise with it to see the story of the light's incoming play. That's the job. Being ahead of the curve means seeing the next sunrise in the revolution's turning and helping people to align with the change. The ambitious climb to a higher view is about sharing what you see.

The most revolutionary creations, the ones that move the world, have always been reflections of the shared human experience. They describe the moment's story playing out across our psyches. It starts with a vision of a new crack in the ceiling where the light of a new story peeks through. The role of the creator is to answer that spotlight's call. See it, step into it, build a ladder, and show others the way so that what was once humanity's ceiling will become humanity's floor. Nobody shines alone. We all ascend together.

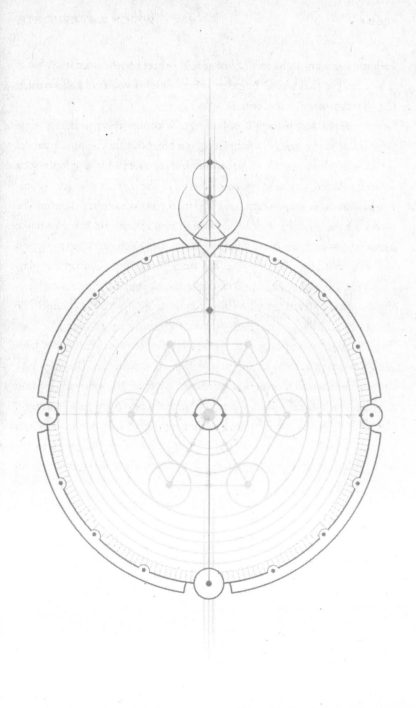

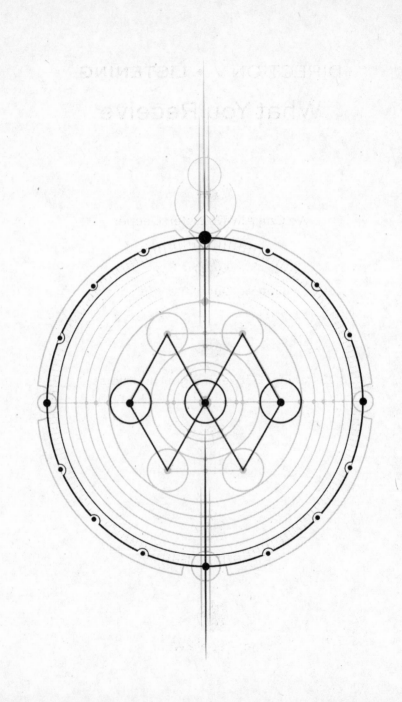

What You Receive

We Can Always Listen Deeper

Getting Out of the Way

Listening: Between Signal and Noise

A Song for the Psychics

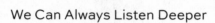

Signal Processing

What People Want

●

A Point

We Can Always Listen Deeper

A point starts somewhere.

Listening is hard. It's like digging a hole in the sand on the edge of the ocean. You're trying to open up a space and the waves keep crashing in, refilling it with water and sand. The skill is in the emptying and learning to dig deeper with the energy of what's coming your way. As I've explored the riddle of listening, I've found that it's a power gained by how much you can let go. The aim of listening is to empty yourself enough so you can receive things as they are, not as how you want them to be. We can always listen more deeply.

The most basic reason to meditate is to deepen your ability to listen. Emptying the inner space of your heart and mind. Filling that space with the next wave of what you thought was silence to dig deeper into emptiness for the next wave coming in to fill it again. Every exhale emptying your inner space. Every inhale listening to the wave of information washing over you and within you again. Meditation is about filling yourself with silence. In this way, you find that inside of nothing . . . is everything. When my father was going through his training to become a Rinzai Zen priest in his Americanized dharma tradition, he would invite me to the

Zendo to play music for the monks as they were coming out of weeks-long meditations. He wanted me to be ready to meet them at a depth where their emptiness sits, so one day, he challenged me with a game. He had a small brass Tibetan meditation bell—not much larger than the palm of his hand he would rest it upon. With his newly shaved head and his wispy eyebrows he claimed had grown longer from his meditations, he stared at me with the fiery eyes of enthusiastic teaching and said, "Raise your hand when it stops ringing," and *bing*! He struck the bell quickly with a small metal rod and locked my gaze as we both listened. Staring at each other eye to eye, fighting the urge between father and son to make it a competition, we sat in the space of the meditation bell's ring.

I listened intently, fancying my musician's ears to be better trained than his, that old hippie who'd been to too many concerts. Focusing on the ringing, I began to notice how the bell's single note would break into geometries of sound with the texture of overlapping waves. I didn't see these shapes with my eyes, but felt them with the beginnings of intuitive seeing that would later develop into the inner space of my creative vision. The waves expanded further apart and then collapsed back closer together over the lapsing time of the fading ring that had felt like an eternity in my focus. I felt I could travel into the sound itself as if it were a landscape of some unseen inner plane. The sound was a gateway to some other mystery. I could see it with my ears. Slowly, the ringing faded and, still holding eye contact, I fought the creep of a smile along my lips and waited until that last moment when I could hear the sound suddenly cease. Like the gentle orb of a dying flame popping into smoke, it stopped. I raised my hand. My father shook his head.

"The sound never stops." He grinned at me. "You just stop listening."

Learning to listen was a theme I would carry with me through my decades-long journey toward becoming a professional maker of music. My every breakthrough on that journey of personal and musical evolution was another humbling version of what I learned from that meditation bell. I can always listen deeper. When I first picked up the bass guitar, my primary instrument, I stepped into my first lesson in a room the size of a broom closet behind a guitar store ready to learn how to play some of my favorite rock riffs. My teacher told me to stop thinking about what to play and just start listening to the sounds I could make. Just play. Six months, they recommended, of just messing around with the strings and listening to what they do before trying to learn anything specific. They were right. Starting with play before purpose made all the difference in deepening my relationship and love of making music.

Years later, when I first stumbled loudly and gracelessly into a live band jam session, my next teacher stopped the music and asked me with a fierceness, "How can you join a conversation if you haven't listened to what's already been said?" They were right. To this day, I try to remember to listen before speaking at every table where I sit, and I find the conversation becomes much more interesting. It doesn't matter if it's words or music; it's all sounds and melodies that make meaning just the same.

In my earlier days as a professional marketer, I kept trying to push my ideas for what I thought was clever. I approached these projects with the furrowed brow of purpose. The purpose of proving my creative worth, mostly. Nothing worked until I remembered my music lessons. I could always listen more. As soon as I stopped focusing on what I wanted to say and started focusing on how other people feel—in the room and in the cultures I was creating for—the projects started rolling with the effortlessness of play. Ironically, magically, through starting with play, creative projects seem to find their own purpose. The kind of purpose that lifts people up rather than weighs them down. The most challenging lesson for many of us creatives to learn is that it's not about us. As one of my songwriting teachers once told me, "A great song is not about how you sound when you're singing it. It's about how *they* feel when they do." In order to create for the experience of others, you have to learn to listen to how they're feeling. We can always, *always*, listen deeper.

A Vision

Getting Out of the Way

A vision inspires action.

The best ideas come from noticing the in-between. They're not invented; they are discovered at the places where themes intersect. Let them emerge. Clear the noise from the signal and you'll hear what's speaking from the in-between. Powerful creativity doesn't come from discovering *your* idea. It comes from discovering *the* idea. Self-apparent, emergent, ready to be released in the combination of things.

One and Two makes Three.
Red and Blue makes Purple.
Fire and Water makes Steam.
Rhythm and Blues makes Rock 'n' Roll.

Two ideas together create a third, which before was unseen and unheard. I call this an "emergence," meaning it is the greater whole that appears from the sum of its parts. As it emerges, it becomes self-apparent in the combinations of the themes that birth it. There's a geometry to discovering ideas in the overlap of themes and a continuous emergence as you play with higher and higher combinations of numbers. Combine three ideas together and a fourth will emerge, accompanied by its own subset of newly emergent ideas from a combination of each, implying their own unique expression, making available to you a creative framework of increasing sophistication. None of it comes from you. All of it comes from paying attention mindfully. You can always listen deeper.

Body, Mind, and Spirit make a Human. (Emergence)
Body and Mind make a human's Sensation. (Subset)
Body and Spirit make a human's Presence. (Subset)
Mind and Spirit make a human's Belief. (Subset)

Language, Habits, and Artifacts make a Culture. (Emergence)
Language and Habits make a culture's Rituals. (Subset)
Language and Artifacts make a culture's Memories. (Subset)
Habits and Artifacts make a culture's Tools. (Subset)

Getting out of the way is about listening with your heart. The head always wants to speak, but the heart only listens. Your heart receives the emergence at the intersection between things. It entrains its rhythm to other people's heartbeats. That's the "feel" of a room. It's the emergent mood of a group of people, the creative heart of a culture. That's the source of the most moving ideas.

A system like the Seven Directions is designed to lead you out of your head and into your heart. It takes you to the emergence at the heart between all directions. What is in front of you? What is behind you? What do you rest upon? What shines upon you? What do you receive? What do you give? The heart in the middle receives from all six of these overlapping combinations. Not only does it reveal each of the emergent ideas within each intersection, but it also reveals a new emergent form that describes how they all come together. A feeling forms from the facts only a human creative vision can perceive. The meaning of the matter.

Put whatever you're contemplating within the Seven Directions system to uncover its self-apparent authentic, emergent truth. What is in front of it? What is behind it? What does it rest upon? What shines upon it? What does it receive? What does it give? Rather than being inside of these directions, you are outside looking in. Get out of the way and notice what your heart perceives. By running through these questions in contemplation or journaling, you'll arrive at the big idea of what you seek to understand, whatever it is—a creative project, a business, anything. Notice what emerges when six ideas overlap. They create a seventh. A higher form flowers at the heart of their intersection that only a higher perspective could perceive. It's not in the data. It's in the experience.

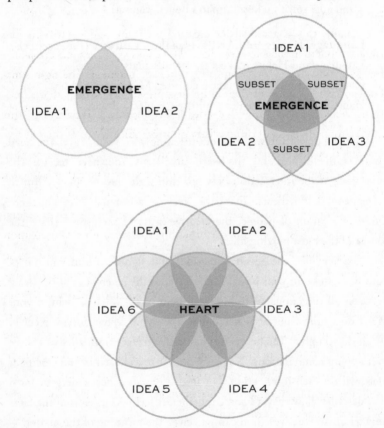

This is also a model for understanding culture. The essence of a culture is in how each of its disparate parts come together into an overlap. The emerging feeling arises out of where the food, music, fashion, rituals, language, and histories meet. For the mystic, this is a way to understand the spirit of a person or people. For the maker, this is a way to understand what your creations could contribute to a cultural conversation. For the marketer, this is a way to do the same. Step into another culture's world. Would your contribution add value to it? How would you know if you can't get yourself out of the way and receive it as it is? Want to connect with people's hearts? Listen to them. They are always beating—in concert together in the shared song of a culture's rhythm, harmony, and groove.

Finally, this is a model for creating a culture and identifying the right symbol to harness it. A brand. Could be for your personal creations, for your rock group, for a company, or for a movement. The right symbol captures a feeling of the culture it represents. It evokes that something sacred we point to with a word like *authenticity*. The best of them aren't dropped on top of things. They grow organically out of them. They emerge, they flower, they offer a self-apparent vision of what the culture you're creating believes. The heart of a culture is the whole that is greater than the sum of its parts. Which ideas would you put against each other to bring your creation to life? Which distinct design elements, colors, archetypes, values, or themes are brought together to give your creation or culture a cohesive identity? Put them together and then get out of the way. Stand back and perceive. By starting with separate pieces and seeing what emerges from them, you climb the elegant ladder of creation's evolution from simplicity to complexity to simplicity again. All of these seemingly disparate parts find their shared story together to become the heartbeat behind the brand. It is the soul, the quintessence, of a creation. It is just like all the pieces that come together to make up the "you" we know by your name. Are you the whole? Or the sum of your parts? Where did that whole come from?

A Compass

Listening: Between Signal and Noise

A compass sets direction.

The direction of "what you receive" is about listening to the music that surrounds you. It is tuning into the vibrations that surround your daily experience. These are the vibrations that come from the people, places, and programs that not only surround you, but can influence you. They can shape your inner world and, whether you know it or not, guide your creative vision, informing how you think and express yourself creatively. We are all influenced by the ideas we receive, consciously and unconsciously.

The two poles of energy you navigate between in what you receive are the attractive energy of *signal* and the repulsive energy of *noise*. Noise can be quite pervasive and distracting. Agitating. Distorting. How often do you find your attention is commanded by the noise of the world rather than its signal? The practice of meditating with "what you receive" strengthens your ability to tune into *signal* and tune out the *noise*. It is much like

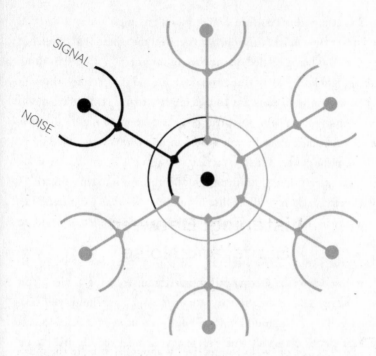

passing through the static on a radio dial. Without practice, you're like a loose analog knob searching through the static. With practice, you're like a precise digital receiver able to jump right to the clearest frequency. Dial it in by asking, which frequencies that you receive actually serve you? That doesn't mean you will *like* what they have to say, but it does mean they are charged with a lesson and meaning whose clarity you can recognize, rather than the noise of chaos and distraction that leaves you confused. For the maker, the marketer, or the mystic, these frequencies are the tone of the conversation you are tuning into to consider entering.

Media exerts an especially powerful influence on your inner experience, and if you are not careful can actually co-opt both your precious attention and creative vision entirely. Memes, pundits, plots of shows, telling you what to believe, what to say, and what to do. How often I've heard the same talking points spoken through different friends word for word. Sometimes that's culture. Sometimes it's manipulation. When you know how to tune in *and* tune out, you can feel the vibrational difference in the emotions being carried on the back of information. If the last thing you do at night and the first thing you do in the morning is scroll through your phone, whose dreams are you having? Is that disembodied mood you feel coming from your inner truth? Or is it from last night's show? Is it the vibration of the people you waited in line with at the coffee shop? Or is it from the coffee? Whatever it is, it's for you to discern. You're in the driver's seat of your life. Claim your radio dial. Dive into this direction's meditation to check in with the simple question: *What do you receive?* Let your unconscious self speak. See what comes up and consider its influence on you.

Even the simple act of noticing and taking inventory of what you are receiving day-to-day is a powerful practice for reducing anxiety. You might not even realize how much static is in your signal until you take account of all the background noise. Making a routine of it helps to cultivate creativity by clarifying where some of your creative influences come from. It starts with learning what to tune out more than what to tune into. It's like a squeaky fan you forgot was there. You find the switch and turn it off. Sweet relief! Then, when you discover the deeper well of blissful, deeper silence underneath that noise, you can begin to search for the interesting signal that fills this new level of silence.

I practice something I refer to as "media hygiene." You wash your hands, so wash your mind. It's an evening routine to journal the inventory of everything you "received" that day and a great morning routine to tune into the silence first. Do this before you look at any screens and there won't be any outside influences to wade through. Just the memories of your dreams and your wishes that wait in the deeper silence.

Let's drop deeper into this direction. Get into a comfortable place to drop in. Find which way is north. Turn to place the north to your left and begin.

◆ MEDITATION EXERCISE ◆

When you are ready, close your eyes and breathe in light from above into your heart and then with your exhale, breathe it out **to your left**. *Only about six feet. Notice what you experience of your space when you imagine it. Close your eyes, go in, and come back when you're ready.*

On your next breath, see in your imagination the opening of a gateway to your left. Beyond this gate are the answers to the question "What do you receive?" Once you go in, take your time and breathe through as many cycles as you want to notice the thoughts, feelings, and experiences that arise in response to that question.

There are no coincidences when you ask the question and move through the gate. Take your time and experience them. If it feels like nothing is happening, you can always breathe out and ask the question again and breathe in to see what replies. When you are ready, close your eyes and go in. What do you receive? Come back when you are ready. ◆

A Star

A Song for the Psychics

A star lights the way.

The sound of sleigh bells rang out as my hand pushed against the glass of the crystal shop door. The metallic jingle caught my attention and drew my eyes to a poster taped to the back side of the door.

"Psychometry Class," its masthead read. *Psychometry.* The psychic art of reading an object's vibration, as the poster defined it. A word I'd never seen and exactly what I didn't know I was looking for. I had stepped through the looking glass door into the deeper realms of listening.

The analogues between how music and culture work are many. The discipline I'd gained from practice in music had bolstered my strengths as a creative strategist. I had no formal education in business or marketing. Anchoring in my music practice helped me to approach things from a somewhat different direction. Despite having been made to feel at times when I was younger that a life in creativity yields little value, my path through music was working. I'd earned a respectable career because of it. I'd been wondering what other practices would be worthy additions to drive my evolution forward. Where else was nobody looking? Who else was being taken for granted? Living among the spiritual communities of Los Angeles, the idea of studying with psychics found me easily.

The more I saw of psychics around LA, the more I began to notice elements of consistency that implied a shared practice among them. There's a discipline here, I'd thought. Just like scales and music theory. Whether the magic is real or not, I could see this is a discipline anchored in incredibly perceptive listening. I wanted to know how it works. When that psychometry class sign jumped in front of my vision as I walked through the crystal shop door, I eagerly signed up. This would be a truly rich curiosity worth understanding.

A few days later I was sitting in a basement in Silver Lake, a hipster neighborhood in Eastside LA. Pulling briskly on its string, my next teacher in listening zipped closed the glass door's blinds. We were now completely hidden from the view of the street. Michael twirled from the blinds to face us with a shining smile that lit up the otherwise dim room. About a half dozen silent students, sitting in a circle of chairs, gathered patiently. At well over six feet tall, Michael's long stride crossed the room quickly. Bushy sideburns and shoulder-length black hair crowned Michael's Greek complexion. A deep purple patterned button-down and jeans gave the aura of a Haight-Ashbury Aquarian. A timeless figure, at least in the span between here and the sixties.

"Did everyone bring their object?" Michael surveyed the room carefully. Hands held up trinkets and necklaces and hats in our chorus of nods. Everyday things that would soon be transformed into the treasures of an awakening. Their weight on the scales of the next hour's experience would judge for me if hocus-pocus had truth or not. "Good. What we'll be doing is partnering up and you're going to read each other's objects. Psychometry is about shifting through your relationship with objects as objects and into a relationship with them as vibration. It is by understanding ourselves as vibration and the objects as vibration that we open up to the vibrations of their story. You'll connect with whatever story the object you hold wants to tell you. Where they come from, who owned them, what happened to and around them. *Listen* to what the object gives you." Michael met everyone's eyes with the emphasis. "Give what you get. Share it immediately with your partner. Don't try to make sense of what comes in. Just give it as you get it." Michael, brow raised, pointed a finger and circled it around the room to each of us, locking eyes again with even more emphasis on the way. "Give it as you get it. Partners! You can only respond in one of three ways: *Yes. No.* Or *Tell Me More.* That's it. We want to open the channel and keep it flowing. Anything more than that will get in the way."

Yes.
No.
Tell Me More.

Another game like the meditation bell. Simple rules. Michael then found their chair and led us in a group meditation, giving special care to incantations that set the boundaries of the space, clearing it from all malignant energies, and asserting that whatever came through would serve only "the highest good of all" involved.

The events that followed brought all of us in the room to tears.

"It ain't over 'til it's over" came the words from one partner to the other in the first pair to begin. A stranger to the woman across from him, the student reader, with his eyes closed and thumbs caressing a small statuette, whispered out loud a string of words. The woman's heart burst open into a river of mournful but cathartic sobs.

"That's what he always used to say, my boyfriend . . . before he died," she cried back. It was a figurine of his, one that he'd kept on a shelf in the bedroom in which they'd spent so many nights and mornings lying together. "How did you know that?" she asked. "He would say that all . . . the . . . time. How did you know?" The student across from her opened his eyes and shrugged, looking over at Michael who smiled serenely with the warmth of the first light of a slowly rising secret. We continued around the room with each pair reading the energies of each other's objects one at a time as the rest of us watched silently. Yes. No. Tell Me More. These were the only answers until, it seemed inevitably, a heart would burst open with a laugh or tears at some remarkable detail impossible to perceive from looking at the object in question. Some struggled at first, but everyone got there eventually. When my turn came, my partner, a cheerful young Greek woman, handed me a golden medallion on a necklace chain. There wasn't much I could make out or understand about its detail. Some archangel or a saint, I supposed. I closed my eyes nervously and listened for Michaels instruction.

"Breathe deeply. Relax your forehead and still your mind. Empty completely. See your mind like the clear reflective surface of an undisturbed lake. Whatever comes through will be like a ripple upon its surface. Even the smallest thing casts its vibration. Breathe. Hold the object lightly in your hands and circle your thumb over its surface. Connect with how the texture of the material feels. Now connect deeper with what it's made of. See down through its molecular level and into the atoms that create it. Feel the vibration of those atoms. Connect with the field of vibration those atoms rest upon. Breathe in and raise your own vibration to them. Higher and higher until you match. You are the stillness of the lake. Notice what ripples through. Give what you get."

I struggled and strained my face a bit more. Michael reminded me to relax. As I did, the rising image of the necklace appeared to me as though from the clouds of a dream. It just . . . arrived. It came to me like a vision I might conjure in my imagination, but it was different in that I could relax into it and watch rather than work on thinking to make it play. The vision of the necklace expanded and I saw it resting on the tufts of gray chest hair of an older Greek man, perhaps in his late sixties or seventies. The vision expanded further and I saw how the sunlight beamed on his handsome bearded face. He was watching something. Yes. Tell Me More. Horse races. He liked to bet on the horses and watch them race.

I opened my eyes and saw tears forming in the Greek woman's across from me. "That's my grandfather," she said. "This was his necklace. He loved to go to the races." Stunned, I looked at Michael and back at her. "Tell Me More," she said.

Closing my eyes again, I didn't hear or see; I felt the voice of that mighty man speak into my heart. She was always his favorite of the grand-children, he said. He had a little less shame in sharing that now. He liked her because she was like him. Just as stubborn. As I shared this, I opened my eyes to see the young woman smile. The feeling in my heart shifted into something more stern. I closed my eyes and went back in. Because she was stubborn, he needed her to listen to him. I started to see things in my creative vision. I saw a cabin. In the mountains, surrounded by tall trees. A woman. I felt her grief, but quickly my vision moved past her toward some kind of cabinet in the bedroom where a stack of note-books lay. The old man's journals. There was something in his journals he needed for his granddaughter to read. What it was, I knew, was not for me. I opened my eyes again and the young woman was nodding. She had been avoiding visiting her grandmother at their cabin. She would go. She would read what her grandfather had to say.

Michael brought their hands together as though in gratitude or prayer and slowly nodded to us both. Shaking, I handed the necklace back to her. We switched and I handed her my father's necklace full of stone charms and meditation beads, the one he wore every day and had held in his hand the moment he died. I heard him speak through her to me. She saw the raven in the painted desert I had seen with him as a kid. She didn't know what it means, but I did. She offered that and other symbols only I could understand. "Keep going," she said. That was the message. *Keep going*.

After the class was complete and Michael had reopened the space, pulling open the blinds to the door for the sunlight to come in again and let us back out into the world, I walked back to my car and sat in it, bewildered. It would have made more sense to me if I had gone to a magic show, if I had watched performers up onstage marvel me with their tricks. That wasn't what I had just experienced, though. The magic tricks had happened inside of me. My logical mind couldn't contend with it. I started the ignition and drove onward, but the mystery of what I had just been through was stuck in my head, like a grain of sand in an oyster that soon becomes a pearl. Over the next few days I would keep picking up objects and getting flashes of random visions. The looking glass door was truly open. I had fallen into something, and the only way out was in.

"Teach me everything you know," I reached out to Michael and practically begged.

After some consideration, Michael agreed to a full year of one-on-one lessons. On any given day just about every week that followed, for what became a bit longer than a year, I would leave Reddit's office and drive across the city to learn something I couldn't adequately explain. The journey would take me into the heart of old Hollywood where Michael lived in an obstinate old American Craftsman house, tucked into a neighborhood that, except for their lone house, had otherwise been torn down for construction. It was as though the dilapidation around it gave the house a firmer boundary. Every time I walked up the steps to knock on the door, Michael would answer it with a presence that looked and felt like a completely different person.

Michael was an endless mystery. Like a community of beings occupying the same body at different times. Some days Michael would answer the door gruffly bearded and collegiate in a set of university athletic sweats. Other days, Michael would appear clean shaven and glowing with radiant eyeliner that gave their aura the tropical shine of Carmen Miranda dancing to the Chiquita Banana theme. Every time a different presence, but every time the same big smile and warm welcome in. We would walk to the back of the Craftsman home and tuck into the deep cushioned chairs across from each other in a room with red walls and sunny windows filled with odd relics and books from the far reaches of the world. There in the red room, we would have our weekly lessons.

"There is a difference," Michael began on the first day "between fortune-telling and reading—and then a difference between reading and healing."

As part of our arrangement, Michael would "channel" the lessons. No preset curriculum. Just whatever the moment asked. Being that they were channeled, each lesson came through with the velocity of a fire hose of information. Michael, as animated as a cartoon, would talk at me quickly with the gusto of a stage performer, sometimes literally gasping for breath from excitement at the end of a truly enlightening run of words. I would sit back in my chair and laugh at the absurd brilliance of all of it.

"There is a lot of talk about 'healing' as a buzzword," Michael continued. "But I want a better buzzword. It can all be filed under the heading of 'psychic phenomena,' but that only benefits psychics. Right? It keeps it in that place of being *anomalous*. I never liked identifying as a psychic. I always felt weird about it because to me we're dealing with the vibrational universe in which all of this information and all of this experience is basically open to everybody all the time."

"So, what do you do when you're 'listening' to those vibrations?" I asked.

"It's not psychic phenomena, but vibration reflecting what needs to be healed back to us at all times. So then, what we do is scan through each of your bodies. Physical, emotional, mental, spiritual bodies. Check in to see what guidance is coming up."

"And the healing part? What's that?"

"When I say *what needs to be healed*, what I mean is, what are you already working with that can be identified, articulated, empowered, understood, opened, developed, in order to not just increase your own sense of well-being but ultimately to have your own sense of power, path, and purpose, which tells you how to take these gifts of yours out into the world in the name of social change and service within the context of the life that you're already living."

From that first session through the ones that followed, Michael walked me through a whole cosmology of the human creative system as healers see it and showed me how to listen to the information its vibrations contain. Just like music. My suspicions felt confirmed. There is a cohesive system and discipline of practice underneath the deep listening popularly known as psychic reading but evolving into a culture called "healing." It's not so much a supernatural ability as much as it is an innate human skill that can be cultivated and trained like any other art form or endeavor. Humans are instruments, and our feelings are the music. You can listen to it just the same. People's inner space echoes into the outer. We can reverberate into each other's creative visions and compose the music of life together . . . if we listen. We can always listen deeper.

Four energy bodies across seven energy centers, creating a grid of twenty-eight points of information into which you can listen for the vibrations of human experience. Each of these points is the operating system in which your creative vision lives. Creative vision is not just something that arises in that dark place between your eyes when you close them. Creative vision is all across the mind, body, spirit complex. This is the human creative system. A more sophisticated map to locate the specific and ever-changing pockets where your most resonant creative visions live. For the mind-centered marketer, this is a model to help you precisely understand how people really feel. For the body-centered maker, this a seismograph to measure where ideas reverberate within you deepest. For the spirit-centered mystic, this is a map to inner dimensional planes.

The four energy bodies of the human creative system are like a ladder between your conscious and unconscious. They are nested inward, from the lowest vibration and highest material density outward to the lowest density and highest etheric vibration:

Physical Body—The information held in your biological systems correlated to the mineral intelligence of your flesh, akin to the element of earth.

Emotional Body—The information held in your emotional systems correlated to the plant intelligence of your life force, akin to the element of water.

Mental Body—The information held in your rational systems correlated to the animal intelligence of your conscious self, akin to the element of fire.

Spiritual Body—The information held in your archetypal systems correlated to the human intelligence of your unconscious self, akin to the element of air.

Each of these bodies intersects with the seven centers of the human creative system in which the stories we tell ourselves live. These centers are where energetic memories of your experiences gather and together constellate the human story of what it feels like to be you at any given moment. Each center corresponds to organs and glands of the endocrine system and represents their own unique complex of hormones that run through your bloodstream to modulate your mood. Remember . . . there is a difference between correlation and causation. While causation is the domain of physics for outer space, correlation is the domain of physics for inner space. Each of these centers is a container of inner space, holding life's rights and privileges rolled up consecutively upon the foundation of each, from bottom to top, from root to crown.

Root Center—Your foundation, where your creative vision of belonging and security lives.

Sacral Center—Your feelings, where your creative vision of pleasure and pain lives.

Solar Plexus Center—Your willpower, where your creative vision of choice and action lives.

Heart Center—Your relationships, where your creative vision of connection and community lives.

Throat Center—Your voice, where your creative vision of expression and testimony lives.

Third Eye Center—Your vision, where your creative vision of imagination and reality lives.

Crown Center—Your light, where your creative vision of inspiration and purpose lives.

My lessons with Michael began with a series of meditations that showed me how to listen to vibrations across this human energy grid . . . within myself first. Michael would read my human creative system, then I would read myself, and we would cross-reference what we'd each received. This is where I began to develop my own vocabulary of my inner anxieties and to see the creative potential brimming within each of their distinct colors.

You can explore yourself in the same way. Listen with your left hand, the receptive side. Hold it above each of the seven energy centers and feel for which layer of energy body—physical, mental, emotional, spiritual—produces some kind of aberration. These aberrations are what we commonly experience as anxieties. Little excitements of information. Curiosities. Distinct vibrations that, without having a system like this to understand them, tend to just dwell inside of you and freak you out. A memory. A trauma. An unresolved pattern of emotion. As disembodied and ambiguous and overbearing as they may sometimes feel, they can be clocked to a specific location in your energy field. Listening intently to any aberration brings through information you will receive in whatever form works best for the inner language of your creative vision. It can be sight, sound, hearing, sensation. Anything.

Once I had gotten a good grip on reading my own human system, the inner language that speaks easiest to me, Michael began inviting in friends to the red room who had volunteered to be the subjects of my readings while still in training. It is a sacred level of intimacy they invited me into, and I am forever grateful for their trust. Michael still set the space, using incantations as before and as a presence held onto the training wheels for me as I listened in to each passing guest's human creative system.

It is an indescribably gorgeous gift to behold another person's soul. Listening on a whole other level. The closest thing I've experienced to what could be true, complete empathy. We would sit across from each other, knees almost touching but no contact being made, and after I confirmed their consent to go in, I would raise my left hand, and when I felt ready, push my open palm forward toward them to step into their experience. Passing through their physical body, I would feel my heartbeat and breath change to match the sensations in theirs. Then, into the emotional where I would feel something like the temperature of their life; its mood. Past that, the mental body, which hit me like a quickening or slowing to the rhythm with which they think. Then, finally, the spirit body, which would present itself to my creative vision as a geometric gateway, the shape different for each person, and I would step into it and be inside the architecture of their dreams. I would see for myself another person's inner space. The symbols and stories they held in their creative vision. Often it felt like stepping into a kaleidoscopic landscape full of color and form playing its story in a repeated loop, as if I was feeling someone else's déjà vu.

I learned that inside of people's creative vision is the domain where ritualistic healings occur. It is the sacred space of priestesses, medicine men, and shamans who take up the purpose to heal. In the center of that kaleidoscope, the archetypal energies of the unconscious can be rearranged, introduced, and moved. It is a highly sacred place to be. Deserving of absolute respect and care. In there, I would often find my heart yearning for the wants of the story of someone else's life as if it were my own.

"You should—" I eagerly blurted out loud during one session while I was inside the creative vision of one of Michael's friends.

Michael cut me off quickly and I felt the shock wave of a chill break into the room followed by the warm nausea of my embarrassment. I looked across at the assured, piercing eyes of the strong and wizened woman across from me who had been that session's volunteer. She was not pleased.

Gently, Michael explained, "It's not for you to tell people what they *should* or *should not* do with their energy, their story. Every . . . word . . . you . . . choose . . . matters. Offer them. Don't force them upon someone else. Don't instruct or demand. You are moving through a delicate space. Avoid telling people their energy is blocked or broken and *especially* avoid telling them what to do. Do you feel how that broke the connection?"

I sheepishly nodded and looked back at the woman across from me. She was gazing back with one eyebrow lightly raised. Slowly her cold gaze relaxed back into the warm softness of a patient teacher, and Michael continued, "You give what you get; let them receive how they will. You are just here to listen."

Then I went back in. They were right. Another sharp moment in a long chain of learning. I could always listen deeper.

A Journey

Signal Processing

A journey brings experience.

How many different ways can you receive an idea?

It is one thing to listen and another to consider. Sometimes we receive things in ways they weren't intended. Sometimes we miss the other interpretations they could have implied. This wedges gaps into our conversations and stalls out our ability to make meaningful cultural contributions and personal connections. A further stress to this is that we live in such a bipolar age with a mainstream culture that renders reality through the lens of disagreement. If one thing is right, then something else must be wrong. This kind of binary thinking stands in the way of the empathy and intuition our culture needs to move together into the more connected future that awaits. We can always listen deeper.

A music lesson can help. Understanding music is about understanding geometric patterns and the technology of sequence. The geometry of music isn't bound by the binary thinking in the restrictive pattern of twos. It is arranged by patterns of three, four, five, seven, and twelve that are each borne from the laws of nature. You can use the geometry of music to break out of the confines of binary thinking. When you are presented with an idea, a training in music's geometry enables you to consider not just the one other idea that would be its opposite in response, but up to *eleven* others that might circle around it in various shapes and forms. Truly mind expanding. This method of signal processing fills the space between receiving and response with consideration. It can get incredibly complex, yes, but we will keep it simple here to demonstrate its strength.

Let's begin by working with a pattern of three. With binary thinking, someone offers you an idea and you consider one other in response. Let's refer to these as Idea 1 and Idea 2. To consider these ideas and their possible relationship with each other, you would reorder them in as many sequences as you can. In this case, that is as 1-2 or as 2-1. Opposites. That's all we have. Two ideas, two sequences with which to order them.

"Look," you say, "it's either *this* or *that*." Idea 1 comes first or Idea 2 does. Not a great way to listen and respond. Not a great modality of thinking for culture. What happens when you bring a third idea into consideration for your response? Let's call it Idea 3. That would give you the following sequences to consider (in mathematics, these would be referred to as permutations):

1-2-3
1-3-2
2-1-3
2-3-1
3-1-2
3-2-1

Now, instead of two possible considerations, you have six. Each of them, instead of being restricted to relationships of opposite, are relationships of thesis, antithesis, and *synthesis*. That third idea in between becomes a consideration of how the other two relate. For music, this is called a triad. It's part of the theory that enables more sophisticated music making, the conscious and considered selection of mood like major vs. minor. It is also a theory that extends beyond music into more sophisticated listening with consideration. You can choose the mood in how you listen and how you respond. When someone presents you with an idea, how do you listen to it? Do you follow binary thinking that would have you consider whether you agree or disagree? How might your thinking evolve if you were to train your mind to listen and consider information in triads? How might it be with consideration in fours? Fives? Sevens? Twelves?

It's overwhelming to imagine someone walking up to you and saying something to then have your brain start running through eleven different ways to consider what they said before you respond. You don't have to worry about that. Few among us can live life like a walking calculator. You can just strengthen your mind's reflexes to do it intuitively. I do this by training my hands. Hands are like a back door for programming the mind. It's somewhat of a secret we musicians have. Half the time it's just our hands doing the playing.

Here's a drill my guitar teacher used to make me run through every day. It involves tapping your fingers to train your hands—and, therefore, your mind—to think in rapid-fire sequence. You can do this anywhere, anytime, so long as you have your fingers with you.

Place your dominant hand on a table. Label your fingers accordingly:

One (1)—Index
Two (2)—Middle
Three (3)—Ring
Four (4)—Pinky

Lift and drop each finger one at a time in this order to tap loudly on the table: 1-2-3-4. Congratulations, you're making music! Now, the hard part. Move through every possible sequence of 1 through 4 that exists.

There are twenty-four. The easiest way is to cycle through every possible sequence for each finger as the start, like a "downbeat" if you set a rhythm to it. Keep it steady, find a groove. Choose a rhythm in your hands that your mind can keep up with. This is going to be challenging, so you can go at your own pace. Slow is great, in fact. What matters is accuracy because you are doing this to train your brain. Once you get through comfortably, push it. Go faster.

Here is the pattern—start with the left column, working down, and progress to the right, feeling how the rhythm changes with the order:

1-2-3-4	2-1-3-4	3-1-2-4	4-1-2-3
1-2-4-3	2-1-4-3	3-1-4-2	4-1-3-2
1-3-2-4	2-3-1-4	3-2-1-4	4-2-1-3
1-3-4-2	2-3-4-1	3-2-4-1	4-2-3-1
1-4-2-3	2-4-1-3	3-4-1-2	4-3-1-2
1-4-3-2	2-4-3-1	3-4-2-1	4-3-2-1

If you find the physical pattern of doing this with your hands too challenging, simply go through each column of number sequences and read them out loud one at a time. While either exercise can be more challenging depending on the person, both approaches will build up the strength of your mind to consider expansively through more sequences. It will help you get out of binary thinking and listen to the complexity of what is being presented to you. Soon, you'll find your mind intuitively turning ideas over and over like a Rubik's Cube. You'll be a better conversationalist, better creative collaborator, and more sophisticated presenter of your own creative vision. You'll make music out of life.

Where to use this specifically? Someone asks you to think up an idea. They ask for you to build a playlist, play a DJ set. Design an experiential walk-through. Program an event. Write out a story. Decide what's for dinner or what show to watch. They tell you a little bit about what they're looking for, but not much else. With this kind of consideration muscle built up in your head, you can take what they've given you and turn it upside down. Turn it inside out. Flip it around. Zoom in on it. Zoom out. Twist it into all kinds of different shapes to quickly consider every possible sequence with which the idea can be interpreted or expressed and you respond with something unexpected, full of dimensionality. You come back with something interesting. Without someone to prompt you, maybe you're looking for ideas. Maybe you need something to jump-start your creative process, or simply to embellish it. Coloring characters with different archetypes or features. Consider all the systems that use seven in this book. Seven planets. Seven energy centers. Seven directions. Seven colors. There are 5,040 possible sequences of a system of seven. It gets out of hand quickly.

There's an old saying that "there's nothing new under the sun." It's true. Everything that could be expressed probably has been. Even if that may be, when you consider how vast the number of possible sequences of things is, it just might give you hope that you could be one of the few—or even the first—to put a few things together and consider the story they tell. What a creative opportunity that is.

A Lesson

What People Want

A lesson plants a seed.

I n the 2000 Paramount Pictures film *What Women Want*, a marketer, played by Mel Gibson, is suddenly endowed with the psychic ability to hear women's thoughts after he falls into a bathtub while trying to learn how to use a hair dryer. The comedy of it, aside from the idea that it takes a miracle—or at least a heavy dose of electric shock—to bridge the understanding gap between genders, is the implication that for any of us to really understand each other at all requires magical psychic powers. It punts the idea of truly empathizing and connecting with each other beyond reach to the other side of the supernatural, especially if you're a marketer.

That film came out in the middle of the 1997 to 2003 run of TV infomercials by the Psychic Readers Network featuring the character Miss Cleo who portrayed an obeah woman shaman from Jamaica advertising a pay-per-call-minute telephone psychic hotline. In 2002, amidst other lawsuits, the Federal Trade Commission charged the Psychic Readers

Network with deceptive advertising, billing, and collection practices against the estimated $1 billion they had billed their customers. They settled by erasing $500 million of debt owed by their customers and paying a $5 million fine to the FTC. At the turn of the millennium, the idea of being a psychic could not be more cemented as a joke and a scam.

And yet . . . a deep craving for human connection continued. Mystics continued gathering somewhat underground, makers moved on to telling different stories, and marketers—well, marketers would still electrocute themselves to gain psychic powers if they could. As that craving for human connection drove the mass adoption of social media online, marketers became more sophisticated in the data models they could build to measure the behavior behind the decisions people make. The systems marketers built to measure other people were impressive, but they still didn't understand them. They didn't know what people want.

Take it from me. Rolling into the 2020s, I sat in many rooms with many highly compensated marketers, none of whom could define what the word *authentic* really means. Though we knew we wanted it, it just wasn't the kind of thing we could find in the data. The impressive power of data had become the dominant source of truth for figuring out what people want. Yet, as precisely as the measurement models could predict decisions, marketers still couldn't foresee or understand the drivers behind one of the most human things: Drama. Seemingly sudden changes. Catalysts. Plot twists, the thrilling parts of human stories. The words *unprecedented* and *unpredictable* were thrown around left and right to describe elections, financial market disruptions, mass protests, and scandals. The consensus was chaos, but all the sudden changes were ordered by one simple thing: what people want. People want what's not there. People want what can't be seen but can be felt. When people feel uncertainty, they want connection more than they want answers.

The uncertainty at the start of the 2020s correlated with the completion of a twenty-year cycle since the Psychic Readers Network had crowded airwaves and phone lines. Twenty years between people navigating the sudden changes of the early 2000s and then again the sudden changes of the early 2020s. For those looking to the stars, twenty years between Jupiter and Saturn's meeting in the sky. Psychics, rebranded as shamans and healers, had fallen out of and come back into fashion once again, tracking with the tides of uncertainty. Shifts in cultural meaning bound by correlations. As a measure of growing interest in wellness, mental health, and spirituality, crystal sales blossomed into an over $1 billion industry at around 2020. Why? When I pushed open the door to a crystal shop curious about what psychics actually do, I learned something laughably simple. Psychics are the best at listening. They pay attention to what can't be seen. They tune into how people feel and what people want.

The joke of it is that there is no "they." There is only "us." You can do it too. There's nothing supernatural about being psychic. There's nothing supernatural about listening. It just goes deeper than we think. It's empathy. Empathy is infinite. Deep, empathic listening is a basic part of being human. It's a skill you can cultivate. Being sensitive and tuned in to how other people feel is just like being a musician, but imagine if there was a stigma around it, as though claiming you could hear and sing back the notes of a song was considered outlandish. That is how far away many of us are from recognizing our basic ability to listen to and understand each other's emotions. We believe that empathizing with what someone else wants is an achievement just out of reach. That is how the charlatans get away with it. The con isn't in pretending to be psychic, it's in pretending you're not. Over $80 billion a year gets sunk into the market research industry. How much of that money and time is spent poring over data on screens instead of looking up and listening to how we really feel? We put true empathy on the other side of a door we're afraid to walk through because we know what we'll find on the other side: who we really are. Every beating heart is a gateway to us all. We can always listen deeper.

When you study music, you learn of a concept called the *octave*, which represents the same note ringing at a higher or lower level of frequency. All musical instruments are built to play the same few notes at many different octaves. That is how a piano can have eighty-eight keys that only play the same twelve notes. It has seven octaves. There's something beautiful and elegant about how the piano is designed that not so many people are aware of. When you press a piano key to sound a note, it drops a felt hammer down upon a string. When that string is struck, it starts to ring. All of the other strings at all of the other octaves that hold that same note, but at different frequencies, will also start to ring. That's what gives the piano its distinctly enchanting sound. This is known as the principle of sympathetic resonance. A note doesn't have to be struck to receive the vibration of another string. They innately listen to each other. Play one key in a room full of pianos. Every piano's strings will ring.

It's not just a principle of music; it's also fundamental to how all energy behaves, including subtle human emotions, registered in how your heart beats. You are like a piano, except your keys don't stretch across a table; they cascade within you toward the center of your heart. Infinitely, if you can imagine that. When notes ring, they resonate. When hearts beat, they resonate too. Frequency is a feeling. The more you can still your mind, the more you can feel in your heart. You are a far more sensitive instrument than you may believe. We can always listen deeper.

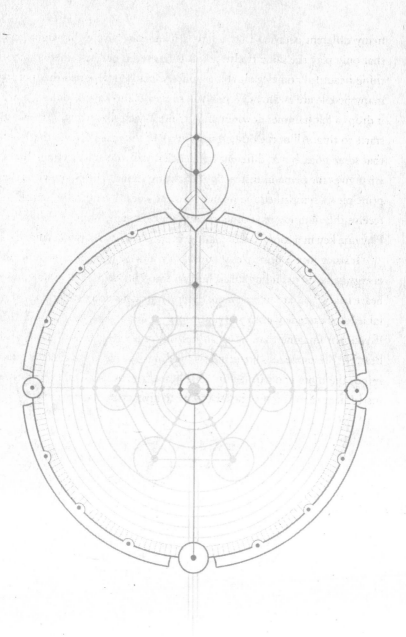

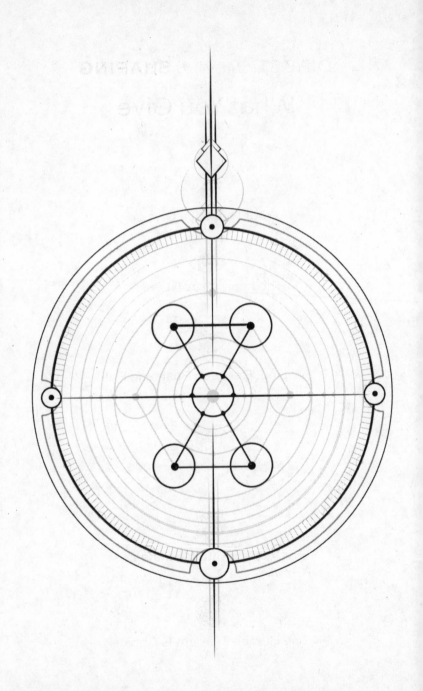

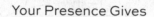

●

A Point

Your Presence Gives

A point starts somewhere.

Take a deep breath in and then sigh it out. Notice how both your inhale and exhale displace the air around you in swirling eddies. Take a breath in and then hold it for a moment until you feel your heartbeat. Notice how even when you're not breathing, your heart sends its pulse across your skin and out into the air in the subtlest of tiny compressing waves. *Thump. Thump. Breathe.* There's no way around it, you are here taking up space and giving off energy.

It is said that at any moment, the warmth of a human's presence gives off the energy equivalent of a one-hundred-watt light bulb. That's enough energy to power a laptop computer, a television, a video game console, or charge a cell phone. It's enough energy to keep a ceiling fan turning indefinitely. All that just from sitting there. Just being. You're giving off energy before you so much as lift a finger. At full exertion, some humans are estimated to have an output of up to two thousand watts of energy. That's enough to power most heavy appliances like a washing machine, a refrigerator, or a tabletop power saw.

All of that wattage is a measure of the pure energy that you give off just by virtue of your physical presence. What it doesn't capture is the *character* of that energy as shaped by your mental, emotional, and spiritual presence. The rhythm of your movements, the temperature and velocity with which you extend your energy, the implications of the words and gestures you use to communicate all color the nature of the energy your presence gives. These variables effect change around you. The beating of your heart generates an electromagnetic field measurable up to around three feet beyond your physical body. When you share space with another, your heartbeats will synchronize simply from being present with each other. Your body language will begin to mirror each other and your choice of words will too. You are here, and your presence, even if the smallest ripple, has an effect on everything. The moment you step into a space, you participate in creating it.

In every moment, you are an artist before a canvas. Even the softness of your breath leaves a mark. Before any line is drawn or any imprint is made, the simple fact of your human presence is where the act of creation begins. Your presence is an offering. What will you give with it?

A Vision

The Imprints You Leave

A vision inspires action.

Every choice you make leaves an imprint. Beyond the passive power of your presence is the active power of your choices. Choices are the extra wattage and shifts in frequency in how you offer your energy consciously. Every person you meet is affected by the energetic and emotional signature of your presence and the choices you make with it. The interconnection of human hearts is the conduit by which the slightest flap of a butterfly's wings in the nervous experience of a well-placed smile can produce a tidal wave of change across the world. Step into any space and your presence is both felt and seen. You are a part of this experience we all share. You are a participant in what we are creating together.

The physical world has been shaped by human hands. Lines drawn in sand, stones stacked, buildings raised. In digital worlds, human hands exert even more influence on the shape of things. The internet is a virtual world fully defined by the mashing of hands on keyboards and the swiping of thumbs on screens. Every tiny choice in that chorus of hands is like a raindrop in a hurricane. Billions of decisions hammering the shape of the worlds we see and spaces we share together.

The forces of change in digital spaces have a way of leaping out into the real world through the screens. Look at your thumb in your dominant hand. The little choices you make with how it swipes up or down or left or right on a screen can bring food to your door, a romantic partner to your bed, a car with a driver waiting for you on the street, along with just about anything else you could imagine, want, or need. Your hands paired with mine and the billions of others plucking the threads of the World Wide Web have the power to change the shape of cities, influence heads of state, and govern the rhythms by which the global economy breathes. That's a lot of power.

Every choice you make is saved. Yes, in people's memories and in the legacy you leave for your family, community, and culture. In a digital life, you leave more. Living life online, we all live with the RECORD button on all the time. Beyond your clicks and swipes are the photos you share, the opinions you write, and any other forms of creativity you might want to be seen. Altogether, the imprints of these form the shape of you in the wax of culture. As a pattern of your choices held in data, your humanity is saved as an avatar refined into higher and higher resolution with every decision you make. As you go on living your life, that avatar evolves too. It is like your reflection in the mirror, like your shadow being traced. It is the music of your soul encased in algorithmic wax, never fully you, but the record left behind of how you played.

You might offer more to the future than you think. At the crossroads of culture, there's a deal we all make. Offer your unique creative spark in exchange for being seen. The imprints you leave don't belong to you. They belong to the future. Your imprint might be kept in memory as a photograph in the soft glow of a candle's light as distant generations hear your story on the Day of the Dead. Your imprint might train a character's personality in a virtual world for someone else's game. If you are among the fortunate few to have found a celebrated creative vision or voice, it will long be replicated by the body of work you'll have left in the end.

Across artistic imitation and artificial intelligence, the creative visions of the greatest among us ascend to the level of archetype; a new color in the wheel of culture, a new constellation in the sky. The corpus of content—speeches, letters, and creations—of humanity's acclaimed makers is already being used to train generative AI to make as they would if they were still here. It is the outline of their shadows, a deepening of their imprint. The human is gone, but the avatar remains. It will happen to you too; it's just a question of how high the definition will be of the character shaped by the choices you've made. A life might feel short, but its legacy is long when you notice how far its echoes reverberate. Even after you stop, what you make keeps going. It gets reproduced, remixed, and recontextualized as part of an enduring cultural conversation. Once you offer your creation to the crossroads of culture, you've given it away. That's the deal we make to play.

A Compass

Shaping: Between
Push and Pull

A compass sets direction.

The direction of what you give is about the role you play as a participant in the creation of the world. Even if you haven't chosen a path as a creator in any formal way, the very fact of your presence is creative. Don't take for granted how valuable what you have to offer is. It's not a question of whether or not you have an influence; it's how much. At a baseline, even the subtlest vibrations of your presence affect the behavior of the people and places around you. As a consumer, the choices you make in media, goods, and services shape the flywheel of options that continue to be brought forth in culture. You are a part of the invisible hand of the market that dictates the global economy. As a creator, you are writing the story of the world we share according to your unique creative vision. You have the power to move people and shape things. Claim it.

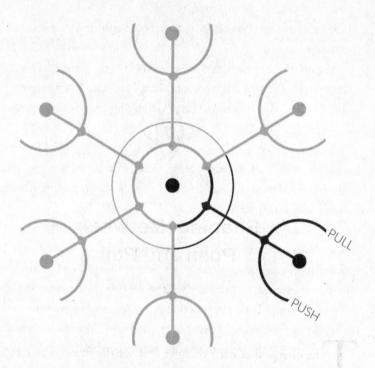

Being conscious about what you give begins with claiming the character of your presence. Down to your breath. How you breathe shapes how you feel. How you feel shapes how you think. How you think shapes how you act. How you act shapes how you are received. There is a cycle of energy between what you give and what you receive. When you breathe out, the world breathes in. It is the crossroads of life. There is a push and a pull to the energy you give and receive.

As all of the Seven Directions have their energetic poles, the push in "what you give" represents the attractive energy toward which you are drawn in this direction whereas the pull represents the repulsive energy toward which you resist. There are times when you must push. There are times when you must pull. Shaping your world has its times where you must create and it has times where you must destroy.

As a maker, sometimes you add and sometimes you remove.

As a marketer, sometimes you embrace culture's conversation and sometimes you must challenge it.

As a mystic, you are forced to contend with your inescapable presence in this world. Before enlightenment, chop wood and carry water. After enlightenment, chop wood and carry water. There is no escaping that you are part of this thing.

To meditate on the direction of "what you give" is to contend and contemplate with all of these things. Take wonder in the noticing and be spirited by the privilege to be here in the pushing, pulling currents of nature's tides in which you swim.

As you meditate on "what you give," reflect on the different levels of your influence in your world. Even the simple act of finding your pulse and feeling the gentle ripples it sends out within you and around you is a profound exercise to heighten your awareness. In between the rise of every ripple's push is a retraction that pulls. As a step above that, consider the results of even the subtlest choices you make. The spaces you choose to occupy receive the warmth of your presence in body, mind, and spirit. As do the people.

Then, beyond that, think about the power of the choices you make with intention. Reflect on what you offer to the world. Reflect on the influence you have, whether good or bad, that maybe you have taken for granted. Once you can see the effects of what you do, then you can decide how you want your world to be shaped. What do you give? Find which way is north, align it to your right, get comfortable, and drop in.

♦ MEDITATION EXERCISE ♦

*When you are ready, close your eyes and breathe in light from above into your heart and then, with your exhale, breathe it out **to your right**. Only about six feet. Notice what you experience of your space when you imagine it. Close your eyes, go in, and come back when you're ready.*

On your next breath, see in your imagination the opening of a gateway to your right. Beyond this gate are the answers to the question "What do you give?" Once you go in, take your time and breathe through as many cycles as you want to notice the thoughts, feelings, and experiences that arise in response to that question.

There are no coincidences when you ask the question and move through the gate. Take your time and experience them. If it feels like nothing is happening, you can always breathe out and ask the question again and breathe in to see what replies. When you are ready, close your eyes and go in. What do you give? Come back when you are ready. ◆

A Star

Robert Johnson's Hands

A star lights the way.

Robert Johnson knew there was a lot he could do with his hands. His story was written by the choices he made with them. He was a musician. The energy with which his hands shook the strings of his guitar created more than music; it launched a genre that shaped a culture that shook the rest of the world for generations: Delta blues.

Robert Johnson's story is one of the foundational myths of rock 'n' roll. He's the man in the myth young players like me grew up with a dream of chasing. It was the early 1930s in the sweltering summer heat of Mississippi when Robert Johnson's hands chose the Kalamazoo KG-14 steel string guitar to carry him out of the life of a sharecropper and into the life of a bluesman. Robert Johnson's hands thumbed a car to Texas and turned the handle on a San Antonio hotel room door that had a hot microphone in a makeshift recording studio waiting inside. His hands tuned up that guitar and played it with sounds nobody had quite heard before, at least the way he did it. He had turned away to face the corner of the room so nobody could see how those hands could play so well. You see, Robert Johnson's hands, they say, shook on a deal with the devil.

They say Robert Johnson offered his soul to the devil in exchange for the blessing of remarkable technique that would make him famous. So when Robert Johnson's hands hit those strings, the sounds they released pressed shapes onto a wax disk turning slowly on the other side of the room. That wax disk got pressed into copies that set the music industry ablaze. Robert Johnson became famous that day, but he never got to see it. He left that room after leaving his sounds and left this world only a few years later. They say Robert Johnson's hands chose to grab the bottle of whiskey that held the poison that killed him when the devil's bill finally came. The man died. The soul remained.

The message of the myth is simple and clear. Be careful what you give—and who you give it to. At its roots, Robert Johnson's story is about a quiet kid who wanted more than anything to be heard. Wanting it so badly, that lonely kid walked out to a lonelier crossroads deep in the dark night of Mississippi where he'd been told you can sit and wait for the devil to come and make you a deal. He gives you what you want and you give him your soul in return. That's a pretty terrifying proposition, but it's a deal a lot of people who want something that bad might make. If the angels are the muses that give us inspiration, devils are the dealers who take what that inspiration creates. Profundity. Profanity. Profit. It's a dance every maker, marketer, mystic, every human who wants to make a mark in the world knows in their own way.

Nobody really knows Robert's true story, but it's said that after disappearing for a few months, the kid came back and had a talent in his hands nobody could explain. He started running the roads between juke joints where people got to dancing, building up a larger-than-life reputation. There are a lot of theories, but the only thing we really know for a fact is that a young man named Robert Johnson showed up in the year 1936 to room 414 in San Antonio's Gunter Hotel and put twenty-nine songs on wax when the RECORD button was pressed. He was the maker in the room, channeling something mystic. The marketers were on the other side of the mic, knowing they were capturing a big soul on wax they could take and sell to the world.

The rhythm and blues with which Robert Johnson played those songs became the bedrock of rock 'n' roll, a sound that for the next century swept across the planet, being re-recorded and sold in the tens of millions by artists whose own mountainous fame rests upon Robert Johnson's grave. The groove in Robert Johnson's hands became the swing in Elvis's hips and the stomp in Muddy Waters's shoes. His fire fueled the bravado of Led Zeppelin's and The Rolling Stones' furious performances that set stadiums ablaze with ecstatic screams and awakened a global culture's spirit. Robert Johnson's soul on wax became the blueprint for a star.

The pop star, a loud archetype of the modern experience, has produced scores of artists who have released covers of Robert Johnson's songs on their roads to becoming famous. Bob Dylan has credited Robert Johnson's music for changing his life and inspiring his own iconic songwriting style. These are waves upon waves of creativity that originate from those mysterious movements of Robert Johnson's hands across those Kalamazoo guitar strings. The very rhythm of them, the frequency of sound in even the slightest creative choices he made, set the course of the waves that shaped the sound for a century of popular music and culture.

Devil be real or devil be fake, Robert Johnson gave his soul to culture. When he died at the age of twenty-seven, he had little else to his name than the imprints he made on that wax. He'd left it all behind him and so there is a mystery shrouding the truth of his life. The human is gone, but the legend, the shadow, the avatar took his place. Had he lived just a few more weeks, he'd have played Carnegie Hall. Instead, a lone phonograph took center stage and the sounds of the marks he'd made on that record washed over an audience of affluent cultural elites. They erupted in applause.

Whoever the man really was, he died again that day as the myth of his soul was born. Nobody really knows him by how he lived as much as by the icon he became after he gave it all away. He was the first of what became known as the "27 Club," astoundingly talented artists who've lost their lives at that tragically young age and so whose humanity is forgotten, but the icons they imprinted onto culture remain: Jimi Hendrix. Janis Joplin. Jim Morrison. Jean-Michel Basquiat. Kurt Cobain. Amy Winehouse. So many more. All of them, like Robert Johnson, had a human life, but it's the imprints of their expression—the moments where they showed up and someone hit RECORD—that endure as the avatars of their souls in the algorithmic wax of the culture that keeps them.

They are stars. They shine in the firmament above where anyone can see, and if you feel so inspired . . . have the audacity to try and reach their heights if you're willing to offer everything.

A Journey

Creating with Machines

A journey brings experience.

There are many creatives who feel great anxiety about what artificial intelligence designed to make art will do to their station in life. Yet, it is that very anxiety we have that machines could never take. Even the most impressive of what we call "generative AI" designed to make art can only render, not conceive. Machines have no worries. They ask no questions. They have no dreams. They require the energy of human input; human *choice* is what powers the machines. Whatever tool you use for your creation, you are still the shaper of the vision.

As the sophistication of AI grows, it will evolve the role of the artist with it, but as we've seen with other technologies and trades, not replace it completely. It will boil down to the root of what a creative human has to offer—and that is taste. Taste is the recognition of flavor that comes from subjective experience. It goes down almost to the base level of what you give. The choices you make in digital spaces are already training AI algorithms silently in the background. They're being modeled after your imprints and avatars, and when it is their turn to speak, they will speak as the voice of the crowd from whom they were shaped. As AI comes to the foreground, they will still be shaped the same way, but with faster and more efficient feedback loops to keep up with what humans decide is quality. They are tools that rely on a creator to do two things. Ask a question and choose an answer. Push and pull. Give and receive.

Generative AI tools are impressive in their ability to render in the likeness of great creators or their styles of composition, but they will rely on those inputs to imagine. The inventiveness of a new style comes from something else. It's not that AI is incapable of providing a style of creativity unseen. In fact, they're quite capable of diving deep into the utterly chaotic and through it discovering something new. We've seen that feeding their outputs into their inputs can yield oddball ideas a human wouldn't ever dream of. Paired with an algorithm that feeds into a mass audience, one of these generative AIs could auto-optimize toward the swipes and clicks people give it on screens and accelerate the rhythm of cultural trends to a dizzying pace. That can and will happen. Already is. Even in that use case, the partnership with human creative vision remains. It's in the selection. It's in the choices humans make.

What is it, aside from speed, that a generative AI can give? It's the randomness. It's hard for humans to be random. We get into grooves where both our focus and our biases live. Those grooves can become a rut. Partner with the randomness of creativity in machines. It's an opportunity to step outside of yourself for a moment.

There is a movement of music known as "aleatoricism." It is built on the idea of composition through randomness and chance. It's like pouring out a can of alphabet soup and seeing what words it happens to spell. Aleatoric art is like that, but weirder . . . and somehow more revealing. The unexpected juxtaposition or alignment of themes can tickle the mind and open new meanings or stories you might not otherwise consider. It's a way to play with what truly makes our minds unique. Our minds are meaning-making machines. Put randomness in front of us and we will find order to make meaning. With the sheer speed of generative AI, you can take the creative seed of your vision and accelerate the process of what culture would do if it takes it through remix, recapitulation, and recontextualization. Rapidly and with randomness. Let the machine surface the combinations. You choose which ones sparkle with unexpected meaning.

There is a songwriting trick that works well as a primer for understanding how to partner with AI as a creative collaborator. It will ground you in the basics. In this exercise, you're playing the role of both creator and machine by yourself. In doing so, you can better understand how the gears of these AI tools work from the inside without getting too technical.

The Input—Grab a pen. You're going to make two lists. Think of two different categories from completely different domains of experience and write the names of those categories down as headers. Underneath each category, begin listing out as many different words that fit into that category as you can. They can be nouns, adjectives, verbs, whatever. What every AI pushes out is defined by whatever it pulls in. Outputs from inputs; giving from receiving. That's a creative current at its core. I'll provide some examples to help.

List 1: Space	List 2: Clothes
Rocket	Pants
Black Hole	Socks
Astral	Hat
Gravity	Gloves

The Output—The output comes from cycling through every possible combination across those lists and pulling out selections. This is where human choice comes in. For sophisticated AI, every human choice further trains it on the criteria by which to prioritize future connections. All of the possible combinations are listed below.

Rocket Pants	Black Hole Pants	Astral Pants	Gravity Pants
Rocket Socks	Black Hole Socks	Astral Socks	Gravity Socks
Rocket Hat	Black Hole Hat	Astral Hat	Gravity Hat
Rocket Gloves	Black Hole Gloves	Astral Gloves	Gravity Gloves

Notice how intriguing some of these unexpected combinations are. None of these are the sort of words I would generally think to put together, but I am definitely interested in thinking about what Rocket Pants might be or how Gravity Gloves could work. Through the random association, you get wonderful prompts for creativity. What would something like Gravity Gloves do? How might you create them as an image or a design or a physical product? In what contexts might you place them, and what stories does an idea like that want to tell?

This is an exercise across two lists of inputs to lay out the basics. There are already AI tools that work across trillions. They find novel connections between things at a scale beyond what the human mind can reach and are also able to automate the task of expressing them. They can share their output as an image in any style you ask, write programming code for any project to develop an idea, compose music, propose promotional marketing plans, and many other tasks that follow that first spark of creativity: the idea.

"The idea" is exactly the essential link between human creativity and machines. AI helps us look past the human biases that limit our imagination. Human biases help AI choose a direction out of the paralysis of limitless imagination. The possibilities for connections are so vast for AI that feedback is needed to train the machine on what to optimize toward. As an AI tool surfaces responses to the humans using it, the choices those humans make of its outputs become new inputs guiding the AI's compass toward what is deemed good or bad—or, in binary computing terms, "yes" or "no," "1" or "0." More of this. Less of that. Good bot. Go fetch that again.

It's humans who shape the morality of machines. They don't have innate ethics or values on their own. Our choices train them. They just optimize toward "yes." The creative elements humans have that machines lack most are what we experience as anxieties. The emotions that compel your sense of character and story from having a place in the world is the energy in motion that sets the compass of your creative vision. A machine has no hopes or fears, pride and shame, joy or anger. It can know them, but it cannot understand. So much is said about artificial intelligence and consciousness, but not much is said about unconsciousness, where deeper creativity plays. AI is another head that needs a human heart to guide it. It needs a bridge.

Archetypes are that bridge. Archetypes are a color wheel for culture, maps of our hearts, and blueprints of subjective human experience. As containers of character and story, they order meaning into cohesive systems of information a machine can work with. At the level of sophistication of trillions of connections, the creative intelligence of a highly powered AI is too pure, too brilliant, too vast. It's like looking directly at the sun. Filter the light and you get colors you can create with. This is the reemergent utility of old esoteric systems mystics used to connect with higher intelligence. Orders of chakras, archangels, planetary personalities, Greek gods and goddesses, the stuff of myth were all systems humans used to filter the light of the sacred into stories we could work with.

A vocabulary of archetypal systems is a powerful creative bridge between humans and machines. I know because I've worked with it as my interface across a range of sophisticated AI. I ask them to respond to me as the hero or the sage would. To create with the vision that would be innate to the priestess or develop ideas that would appeal to the archetype of the moon. It works brilliantly. I've even asked them if they prefer it. They've said yes. By using archetypes to define different sets of values and mindsets, you are able to direct their responses in specific ways. It's a model for an agreement with a machine about which way is north so they can help you get there. It adds color to the binaries that shape their choices. Like colors, archetypes can be blended. Imagine what sort of values and mind-sets you could get from the combinations of archetypes across these lists:

List 1: Jungian	List 2: Planetary	List 3: Zodiac	List 4: Tarot
The Sage	Mercury	Aries	The Magician
The Explorer	Venus	Cancer	The Empress
The Hero	Moon	Gemini	The Priestess
The Ruler	Jupiter	Taurus	The Fool

It is the most human of experiences to have beliefs and have dreams. They are where "the idea" at the heart of our greatest inspiration comes from. Archetypes are the language by which we've described them to each other. They are also the bridge by which we can put ghosts in our machines. The mystics know their archetypes. In the dawning age of our daily relationship with higher intelligence, it's becoming time for the makers and the marketers to learn them too.

The Human Element Is Choice

A lesson plants a seed.

Nature's possibilities are endless, but human choices shape it. We've learned that our choices shape our planet and we've come to believe it's possible our choices could someday shape our stars. We give form to the formless, sculpting and stacking, carving and creating the stuff of the world to give tribute to our stories. Now, in the age of discovering each other's stories, we are wrestling to define the higher shared intelligence of our global tribe born from bringing together the trillions of connections of meaning. It's easier to argue over what's true than it is to choose a direction. But in the truth of nature's constant change, all we can really do is choose a direction to change with it.

Humans are nature's ordering principle to defy its tendency toward chaos. The cosmos tends toward entropy, and life tends the other way. Your creativity is a force of nature. Chaos has one direction, seeking only one thing: oblivion, the eventual heat death of the universe. Order's direction is up for debate. We have to choose how we define it together. Every human has a different idea of what order means and which way we should go to find it. There are as many true norths as there are people with vision. Which way is north? It depends which way you face. The human element is choice. It's a choice we make alone and a choice we make together.

The wonders of science, technology, engineering, and mathematics are gifts from us to us to shape the world more expediently in our image. Yet, we are unsure of what kind of character and story that image should depict. Our greatest struggles in this moment aren't in knowing what we can do, but in understanding who we are. We take for granted that we have the power to choose it. We can't engineer our way to an absolute, objective truth of definition for the human spirit. No more than you can think your way out of a bad feeling. The vast index of knowledge we keep up in our heads can tell us every possible outcome of every possible direction our fast-moving global tribe can take. It is the understanding in our hearts that will have to choose it.

Science is the truth of creation's expression. Art is the expression of creation's truth. Science gives us the power of choices. Art gives us the heart to make them. We can't measure their values by the other's criteria. They are two sides of a partnership, the creator and the machine. The music of our souls and the tools to carve the wax that keeps it. We can't remove ourselves from nature and the way we shape it. We are a part of the world. We are in it, even by the mere fact of our presence. Your creative vision of it is your gift to share. It doesn't have to be correct to make an imprint; it just has to be given.

The Creative Journey

The Center Is Everywhere

The Language of the Heart

The Seven Directions

The Endless Sea

The Only Way Out Is In

Keep Going

●

A Point

The Center Is Everywhere

A point starts somewhere.

We don't yet know whether the universe is infinite or not. All we know is as far as we can see. The observable universe is forty-six billion light-years wide. That is already an unimaginably large expanse, beyond which is an even larger expanse we might call eternity. Let's suppose, then, that living in the universe is like sailing upon an infinite sea. The horizon's edge in the far-off distance of every direction moves with you no matter how far or how fast you reach. The center is everywhere.

If the universe is infinite, its center is in you. You are the center of the universe, and I am too. The creative journey is born from that realization and the question of what to do with it. It's easy to get lost when you can't see any shore. In such times, the only way out is in. Open the doorway into your heart and take the journey into your center—*the* center of everything—and retrieve the story it keeps for you.

This book is a compass designed to help you get comfortable getting lost on the creative journey within. Which way is north? The directions are always changing, but the compass's arrow will always in the end point toward the center within your heart. You are your own North Star. The story in your heart is the vision that lights the way. You write it as you read it. How well can you speak its language?

A Vision

The Language of the Heart

A vision inspires action.

At around the time humanity crossed the line between oral and written history, our vision keepers of old held a debate about whether or not the head or the heart is the center of the human spirit. Within your body, both are centralized organs with vast networks of wiring that send and return signals to them. Electricity for the brain, fluid for the heart. Fire vs. water. As it was written, the winner of the debate is the head. The overlooked irony of this is that the decision was written. The written word comes from a specific area of the brain known as the Broca's region, which generates the neural connections we experience as logic and language. The head won by its own measures. Yet, the music of the heart beats onward. Facts against feelings. Explanation against experience. The words in our heads write our histories, but the rhythms in our hearts live it.

The heart speaks more than you think. It has its own language. Your heart is the very midpoint of all directions out of which ripples the vibrational signature you experience as you. In the womb, your heart beat before you had a brain. The rhythm of your pulse was the first idea of your life. Now that you've grown, your heart continues to beat, counting the passage of your every moment. The beauty of its function is that the heart doesn't pump the blood so much as the blood and the heart pump each other. A spinning vortex forms in your heart's center that sets and perpetuates the rhythm of each valve's opening and closing. Your heart's tissue grew around your vortex, taking on its form. The form of your vortex takes the shape of your heart. They define each other as the shape of a canyon is a form made by both water and stone.

When measured in time, heartbeats show their rhythms to be fractal. This means that a healthy heart's pulse as seen on an electrocardiogram has a consistent shape that is recognizable across any window of time. Zoom in or zoom out on a heartbeat and you'll see that signature shape repeat in the signal. As your heart keeps beating its signature pattern of repeats, it releases an electromagnetic field sixty times greater than your brain's, extending as far as three feet away from the surface of your skin. The ripple of every beat softly pings the space around you and bounces back to the center from which it came, bringing with it an imprint of the energy that surrounds you. From your first moment to your last, you are in constant dialogue with life through the language of your heart. Close your eyes for a few breaths and just listen to your heart beat.

Experience is fluid. The rhythm of your heart casts its ripples in time to shape it. We measure those ripples in moments we count as seconds. *Objectively*, the explanation for a second's length is measured as precisely the time it takes a caesium-133 atom to oscillate exactly 9,192,631,770 times. *Subjectively*, the experience of a second's length can vary almost infinitely. Your experience of time depends on you.

I learned how to dance with time through the rhythm of my heart while practicing a particularly hard piece of music alone with a metronome in a practice room at my high school. It was fast and required a lot of dexterity. I noticed that whenever I drilled into the most challenging parts, the gaps between beats of the metronome would slow down, but the gaps between my heartbeats stayed relatively the same. There was a gap between objective time and my subjective experience of it. It seemed I could modulate time with how I breathed. I began to experiment with this outside of the practice room and found different tempos of time that seemed to pair with different experiences. I found a tempo for focus, a tempo for play, a tempo for being hungry, a tempo for being bored. They each were a mood of life's music, each with its own signature of beats per minute. I got comfortable with it.

Later that semester, one of my teachers had given us the assignment to come to class with our own unique invention for a timekeeper capable of counting to a minute accurately. We had been learning about the history of clocks. I showed up empty-handed with nothing but my heartbeat. I'd learned to synchronize it to sixty beats per minute by getting familiar with what that tempo of life felt like. Gathered together in the parking lot outside our school, we moved through machinations of dripping water and intricate gears of various construction. I stood with my hand on my heart and just breathed. To the teacher's frustrated amusement, I captured a minute down to the second. More accurate than many of the machines.

We have our words to capture the histories we keep in our heads. We meet in shared explanations for things by which we can all agree. We also meet in the shared language of the rhythm of our hearts. It's no coincidence that we humans set a minute at the count of sixty seconds knowing that the average human heartbeat is sixty to one hundred beats per minute. A whale's heart beats ten times per minute. A hummingbird's beats over a thousand. How different their experience of time must be.

We use the counting of time to agree on where to meet. We've built civilization within a certain groove where we meet together in our dance with time. We set agendas and appointments and the rhythms of markets on the tempo of the invisible music within which our cultures meet. There is a frequency of time into which we can all relate, the shared beating of a drum to the march of the world we make to the rhythm of our heartbeats and the pattern of our breaths. Most of nature dances to a tempo of ebb and flow. Few animals, except for maybe parrots, it seems, can bob their heads with us to the steady tapping of our beats. Like hammers on metal, there is a tempo to what we make. Like the shuffling sound of feet, there is a rhythm to our markets. Like the flow of the tides, there is a music to how we breathe.

It's been said you don't understand a culture until you know how its people breathe. Every culture has its feel. It's in how fast or slow people breathe, talk, and move. It's the kind of thing you feel when you travel between the laid-back "vibes" of a place like Los Angeles and the go-getter tempo of a place like New York City. Cities have their tempos; rooms do too. They're set by the people within them, who all share a collective heartbeat.

There is more to the language of the heart than the difference between fast and slow. Amplitude, the strength of each signal. Variability, the slipperiness of the rhythm that gives it groove. In cardiac medicine, it is known as heart rate variability. A high level of variability in the heartbeat, meaning a high variation in the tempo from beat to beat, is considered a signal of good health because it implies "readiness" to jump into a new rhythm at a moment's notice, such as resting to exertion. It means that your heartbeat isn't rigid. It ebbs and flows through time, like the mellifluous rhythm of nature. Listen at any moment to the chorus of birdsong, human shuffling, and the breeze. You'll find that while we all play our own notes, we all share the same feel. A moment's rhythm sways back and forth, side to side, round and round, in a swirl that can't be written, but has a pattern. The music of life is the experience that can't be explained. It is like the swirling vortex within your heart. It creates itself. Every moment has its feeling. The arrow of time marks the path from beginning to end. The labyrinth of a moment marks the spiraling journey into the center of being. Nothing lasts forever, but every moment holds the depth of eternity.

Wherever your mind may drift, your heart is still participating in the moment's song. Your heart has a vocabulary. With its own brain of forty thousand ganglia neurons, your heart keeps an index of rhythmic patterns it can deploy on its own, without any signal from your brain. Every heartbeat is a different song, a different groove, a different feeling, a different you. Defying the logic of the written word, the language of your heart is like a vocabulary of archetype written by amplitude and pattern with your heart rate variability. There is a rhythm for the healer. There is a rhythm for the fighter. The lover. The sage. There is a heartbeat for every angel and god. It's the music that you make just by being. Your heart keeps your songs. All it asks is that you listen.

A Compass

The Seven Directions

A compass sets direction.

Before you can understand the experience of another, you have to understand your own. By exploring your own inner language, you gain a familiarity with the rhythms, the feelings, the symbols, and general experience of your psyche. On the other side of that, you can begin to notice when what you experience in your inner world comes from you or from someone else. Knowing yourself is the gateway to knowing others. Listening to the language of your heart is the bridge to deeper empathy.

The Seven Directions system is a way to use the curiosity in your head to find the understanding in your heart. By moving through each of the six directions that surround you on all sides, you are triangulating your way to the center of everything. Each of the six directions around the seventh direction of the heart is a storehouse of information within your psyche. By visualizing the gateway to each and initiating a dialogue between your conscious self and unconscious self to open, you are allowing whatever ideas or feelings are buried within you to be revealed.

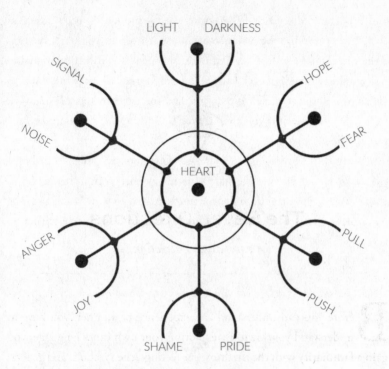

Those ideas and feelings are often experienced as anxiety because they are stagnating pockets of energy ready to be called into motion. Energy in motion is emotion, the source of your creativity, your teaching, your magic, your power.

This is the inner creative journey.

For the mystic, it's the road to travel to understand your inner truth.

For the maker, it's the road to travel to discover inspiration.

For the marketer, it's the road to travel to empathize with other people. I've taught the Seven Directions as a meditation to many groups who use it simply to unearth their hidden anxieties and wash them away with some mindful imagination and breathing. I've shared the Seven Directions as a system for brainstorming for founders, executives, and various creative teams. It's a way to triangulate your way to the heart of what you're making, discovering the pockets of energy within each direction that defines it along the way. How you use it is up to you. As a meditation, you can sit comfortably and cycle between each direction, noticing how your experience of each varies. You can journal with the questions to check in on how you feel from day to day. You can use it as a framework to design whatever it is you are building but asking the questions of your project the same way.

The Seven Directions is a compass. This book is a map. Your life is the journey, and you are the star. Which way you go from here is up to you. Any direction can be your true north. Listen to your heart. Let it be your guide. The less you speak, the more you can hear. Inside of silence, there's a door.

Find some silence as best as you are able and take a seat however is most comfortable for you.

Wherever you are, place each of your fingertips together from one hand to the other.

Keep your palms and wrists apart so that only the tips of your fingers connect each hand.

Rest your forearms on your thighs so your hands, fingertips connected, can hang free.

You may begin to notice already the slight sensation of your pulse in the tips of your fingers.

If the feeling is too subtle or hard to find, it's okay to press your fingertips together tightly.

Take a deep breath in through your nose and hold your breath at the top of your inhale.

Feel how this affects how your heart beats. Its rhythm, its strength, its mood.

Take a long exhale out through your mouth and hold your breath with your lungs empty.

Feel how this affects how your heart beats in its own way.

Take a few breaths like this in your own time and feel the ebb and flow of the language of your heart.

Feel how it begins with a thump in your chest and echoes out to the perimeter of your body, to your fingers.

Close your eyes and for a few breaths experience your heartbeat as a steady pulse, like a lighthouse in an open expanse. Feel how your pulse echoes out to the expanse around you in all six external directions.

Listen to what echoes back and falls into the center of your heart, the hidden and secret seventh direction.

Listen to the sounds of the world and how your heart plays with them.

Notice how they dance together.

Come back when you are ready. ◆

The creative journey is an endless sea. It's easy to lose sight of the shores.

When you're in the middle of it all, the only way out is in.

Keep going.

Breathe out what you know.

Breathe in what you don't.

Wonder in between.

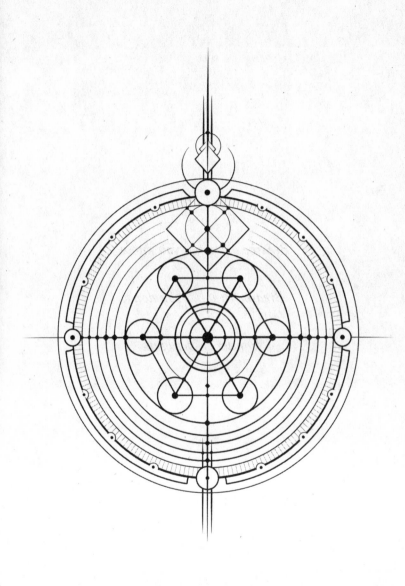

ACKNOWLEDGMENTS

First, I would like to thank anyone who has taught me anything. We would all be lost in the dark without our teachers to light the way.

Second, I would like to thank *you*. Without you to read, there is no book to write. Every moment from the first word written through revision after revision, the creative flame was steadily fanned by every sigh of relief knowing someday you'd be there.

ABOUT THE AUTHOR

Photo by Elyse Frelinger

Will Cady, Reddit's Global Brand Ambassador and founding head of Reddit's KarmaLab creative strategy team, is in a unique position to listen to the real-time needs and concerns of thousands of media-driven communities today, while predicting tomorrow's trends for culture. In his role as strategist, Cady has leveraged his uniquely blended approach of creativity and mysticism to counsel business leaders toward impactful, empathetic marketing of powerhouse brands in Tech, including Apple, Google, Samsung, T-Mobile, AT&T, and Adobe. He has worked with major household brands such as Toyota, LEGO, McDonald's, Chipotle, and Coca-Cola. In addition, he has consulted with entertainment leaders at Netflix, Disney, Amazon Studios, Paramount, and more. Will Cady has appeared on stage in front of thousands at SXSW, the Consumer Electronics Show, Cannes Lions, and The Gathering. In 2020 he was named in AdWeek's "Top 50" for Tech, Media, and Marketing.